CHALLENGES
in **Prayer**

CHALLENGES in Prayer

A CLASSIC WITH A NEW INTRODUCTION

M. Basil Pennington

Liguori
LIGUORI, MISSOURI

Imprimi Potest: Thomas D. Picton, C.Ss.R.
Provincial, Denver Province, The Redemptorists

Published by Liguori Publications
Liguori, Missouri
www.liguori.org

Originally published in 1982 by Michael Glazier, Inc., 1723 Delaware Avenue, Wilmington, Delaware, and Dominican Publications, Sr. Saviours, Dublin, Ireland.

Library of Congress Cataloging-in-Publication Data

Pennington, M. Basil.
    Challenges in prayer : a classic with a new introduction / M. Basil Pennington.—Rev. ed.
        p. cm.
    Includes bibliographical references.
    ISBN 0-7648-1344-7
    1. Prayer—Catholic Church. I. Title.

BV215.P455 2005
248.3'2—dc22   2005051359

Liguori Publications, a nonprofit corporation, is an apostolate of the Redemptorists. To learn more about the Redemptorists, visit *Redemptorists.com.*

Printed in the United States of America
09 08 07 06 05   5 4 3 2 1
Revised edition 2005

In tribute to
a great spiritual father
and
teacher of prayer,
Dom Eugene Boylan

Contents

Welcome • ix

Why Pray? • 1

How Should We Pray? • 11

Time Is of the Essence • 19

The Journey • 29

In the Desert—Dryness • 37

Those Darn Distractions—Bless Them! • 43

Making Intercession • 51

Praise the Lord! • 59

Who Is a Contemplative? • 69

The Contemplative Attitude • 77

Jesus, Our Teacher of Prayer • 89

Mary, Teach Us How to Pray • 97

Appendixes • 107

Welcome

This volume came out of an encounter with a jovial Irishman, a witty and happy man, who was just completing a very successful career as a publisher of legal works. It was in the crypt of the National Shrine of the Immaculate Conception where I was conducting a day of prayer. The invigorating waves of the Second Vatican Council were sweeping across our land. A liturgical renewal was nourishing a renewed Catholic life. Interest in prayer was in ascendancy. Michael Glazier, my Irishman, who had been publishing history and law, had decided before he would put the shutters on his printing establishment and retire, he would turn his hand to religious publishing for a bit, at least to publish a few oldies he longed to see again in print. The response was more than heartening. He found that there was a veritable hunger and thirst for such writings. The packed crowd in the crypt of the shrine on that day told him even more. The people of God longed for good teaching on prayer, good practical teaching. Before that day was out plans were underway for a new series, the first of a number of series this good man would publish to feed God's people. I willingly agreed to edit the new series, *Ways of Prayer*, and promised to prepare the first volume, *Challenges in Prayer*. It was not long before this volume saw the light of day.

As Mr. Glazier had planned it, this volume is meant to be

practical as well as informational. It seeks to pass along the living tradition in a way that it can come to life in "today's and tomorrow's Christian community." After serving well "today's," through the 1980s and 1990s, it now comes to "tomorrow's," the people of God of the twenty-first century—a people, it seems, even more enthusiastic about prayer and eager to partake in the tradition that is rightly their heritage.

The greatest challenge for us moderns is time. We will make time for prayer, precious and significant time in prime time, only if we are really convinced of the value of prayer for ourselves, for those we love, and for the fulfillment of our lives in God. The contemplative Baptist theologian, Glenn Hinson, likes to share a story from his early days as a professor at the Baptist seminary in Louisville, Kentucky. In what was a very audacious undertaking in those pre-Vatican II days, Professor Hinson took a group of his students to visit the Cistercian monks at Gethsemane Abbey, which is not far from Louisville. Father Louis was asked to be their guide. They did not recognize him to be Thomas Merton, the author whose autobiography was a bestseller at that time. At the end of their tour, as Father Louis was answering questions, with the frankness of the young, one of the seminarians asked the monk, "What is a smart guy like you doing holed up in a place like this?" Merton replied very simply, "I believe in the power of prayer." Hinson goes on to say that as he drove home that day and in the following days he kept asking himself, *Do I believe in the power of prayer?*

Do I believe in the power of prayer? It is a matter of faith. And as Saint Paul tells us, "Faith comes through hearing." Here is the importance of the Liturgy of the Word, the gathering of the people of God to hear the Word of God. In those pre-Vatican II days

Catholics for the most part failed to appreciate this. It was something we had to learn from our brethren in the other churches. Certainly a big part of the renewal for Catholics has been the renewal of the Liturgy of the Word, both at the eucharistic celebration and in the celebration of the other sacraments, as well as in almost any gathering of the faithful today. Of course it is very important that when we do gather for the Liturgy of the Word we really do listen and hear, lest there is directed towards us those words of Jesus: "They have ears and hear not."

In practice we need more than this communal hearing of the word. In the realization of this, there has been also a very strong renewal of the traditional practice of *Lectio Divina. Lectio* is not so much a reading of Scripture as a hearing, letting God here and now speak to us through the inspired word. It is important when we come to *Lectio Divina* that we have a real sense of coming into presence. God is truly present in the inspired word. And we want to call upon the Holy Spirit, for Jesus assured us that it would be the Holy Spirit, the Paraclete, who would teach us and help us to understand all that Jesus taught us. With this little preparation, we begin to listen, to let the Lord speak to us in and through the words of revelation, to give us that personal revelation that will nurture our faith, make it more actual, making us want a deeper communion with our God. While there is a chapter on *Lectio* in this volume, we have added in an appendix a practical method of *Lectio* that many have found useful.

We have also added a traditional, practical, simple method to enter into contemplative prayer, presently called centering prayer. I do not believe we have yet passed fully beyond the crippling belief that contemplation is for a privileged few. As we moved into the era when the desire for more contemplative experience was being more widely recognized among the people of God, practical methods of a contemplative nature from the other great religious traditions were being more widely shared in Christian countries. These were appreciated and used by many Christians with varying degrees of understanding and success in integrating them into a Christian theological perspective. But sad to say there was a widespread ignorance of the Christian tradition and there still is. Many, even Christians, labor under the misconception that one must go to the Hindus or Buddhists to learn to meditate in a contemplative way. Fortunately with the development and growth of the *Contemplative Outreach, Ltd.* and the diffusion of the teaching of centering prayer and the ancient Christian tradition of which it is an expression, this ignorance and misconception is being dissipated.

A good bit of concise teaching on the ways of prayer is packed into this slender volume. However, it remains hardly more than an introductory primer. Perhaps that is all many need, for it is truly the Holy Spirit who teaches us to pray. The learning is in the doing. We do seek to offer some further help by adding a brief Suggested Reading section that might well supplement this volume.

The general brevity of the teaching here has allowed for only a very meager manifestation of the very rich and beautiful Marian dimension of Christian prayer. This will be found more fully in some of the volumes suggested. I must confess I am tempted to fall back on a popular medieval adage: *De Maria numquam satis—* Of Mary we can never say enough. This is perhaps more the lover than the theologian speaking, but I daresay it finds its echo in the heart of every lover of Christ for he or she is a child of Mary. In her seven reported utterances in the gospels, Mary gives us a very complete lesson on how to pray; indeed, on how to live a perfect Christian life.

May I add a final word of advice, which comes from a great spiritual father, Dom Chapman: "Pray as you can, don't pray as you can't." Do not let any preconceived ideas form or shape your communion with your divine Friend—what sister said or what mother did. Don't hesitate or be afraid to try different ways to hear the Lord, to be with the Lord, to communicate to the Lord. In a sense only you can be the judge of what really works for you. This is not to deny the great value of having a companion for the journey, someone with whom you can confidently share even what is most intimate. Such persons can not only support us in our fidelity to giving ourselves wholehearted to cultivating our relationship with God in Christ, but they can help us to keep an appropriate objectivity within a most intimate inter-subjective relationship. In the end, prayer is between two persons, you and a God who is Love, in a union of love that is ever growing, reaching to oneness that is beyond anything we can conceive. It certainly is an adventure that has its vicissitudes and challenges and its moments of joy that touch on the very borders of heaven.

ABBA BASIL
FEBRUARY 23, 2005

Why Pray?

I really never like to speak before an audience of any size. I feel very uncomfortable for fear that, not knowing the persons who make up my audience, I may very well be bringing coals to Newcastle. All that I have to say may already be well known to my listeners. Their questions might be wholly other. And now, as I begin this, I feel very much the same. I do not know what the questions, the hopes, or the expectations are that you bring as you begin to read. What then?

Once, when I was still a novice, our redheaded prior, who had more than a bit of the devil in him, started off his morning chapter talk with the announcement: "I want you to listen very carefully today, for I have something very important for you to hear." He went on to give a rather run-of-the-mill talk, whose topic I cannot even remember. At the end of the talk, with a rather mischievous twinkle in his eye, he said, "Well, now, I hope you haven't missed the very important word I had for you today. For Saint Teresa has told us that in every sermon, if we listen with faith, the Lord will have a special word for us."

Needless to say, the brethren, including myself, felt we had been taken in. Yet his word is true. If we come with faith, seeking, there is a word of life for us. And I do think that conviction is implicit in our hope as we reach again and again for books on prayer. Whoever the author may be, we hope that through him will come some word that will help us in our quest to understand prayer, to perceive more deeply its meaning in our lives. We want to be more strongly motivated so that we will be more faithful. We want to experience the fruits of prayer that we have heard so much about. Later we will come back to the question of our wants and desires. For now let us return simply to the question: "Why?"—why pray, why should I pray, why do I pray?

I do not know if it is necessary to say anything really new here, or if that is even possible. Our novices have four conferences a week with their Father Master. These conferences have been traditionally referred to as "repetitions." Certainly if the novice master has been in office for any length of time he has said it all before. But probably it is also true that most of what he has to say the novices have heard before. But newness of matter is not the issue. It is rather a newness of mind and heart that we seek—that the Spirit, who has been sent to dwell in us to teach us all things, might break through the clouds and send a shaft of vibrant, penetrating, enlivening light, so that the old truth becomes a new life-giving insight for us. It is with great dependence on the Holy Spirit that I would like us to go ahead in this sharing on prayer.

I made a little bookshelf last week. I took some planed wood off the pile, measured it, sawed it up, put the pieces together, sanded the rough edges, stained it a dark walnut and set it in its appointed place. Only now as I write this do I pause to look at it in the nitch under the little gas stove. It has done very well all week without me.

God made you and he made me. Is it quite the same? Did he put us together and then go about his business, perhaps occasionally taking a look to see how we were surviving? Is that why we pray—to get him to take a look, and perhaps add a few of the finishing touches we feel in need of, or to repair some of the damage we have sustained?

Not at all. The case is quite different. When I made my bookcase I took some lumber on hand. The lumber already had existence. All I did was to transform its shape and appearance in various ways. When God makes something, he really "begins from scratch." When God made the first human he may well have used a bit of red clay or just some plain old mud, but where did the mud, the lumber, come from—and all the energy, skill, and design? Ultimately, it all comes from God.

One day a rich young man ran up to our Lord and said, "Good Master, what must I do to gain eternal life?" Our Lord answered, "Why do you call me good? One is good—God." One is good—God. And everything that is, is good. For to be is to be good. Everything that is, is of God, of his goodness. When we create, we merely take in hand some existing material and give it new form or shape. Not so with God. When he creates he brings forth out of nothing. He uses no previously existing material, but rather shares something of his own superabundant being and goodness. Indeed, at every moment he is sharing, he is allowing us to participate in his being and goodness. So he does not make us and then walk away and leave us to fend for ourselves. Every moment he is present to his creature, to each created person and thing, bringing it forth into being through a sharing in his being. If we truly see things, if we truly see ourselves, we see God. At the depth of our being, at the ground, the root, God is always there, bringing us forth in his love. "In him we live and move and have our being" (Acts 17:28).

This is indeed a fundamental reason why we should pray. This constant presence, this constant gift—the gift of ourselves and of all that is—demands a response, a response of overwhelming and stunned gratitude. "If you but knew the gift of God!"

But it does not end there. That is only the beginning—the absolutely essential and utterly incomprehensible beginning—but only the beginning. There is so much more. For we have been baptized into Christ. In some mysterious way we are Christ. "It is no longer I who live, but it is Christ who lives in me" (Galatians 2:20). We are in some way far beyond our comprehending, one with Christ, the very son of God. We are one with the Son, coming forth from the Father, returning to the Father in that perfect love who is the Holy Spirit. The Holy Spirit has been given to us as our Spirit. He is our Spirit. He is Gift, and he has been given to us. When we get down to it, *we are prayer.* We are the Son, to the Father, in the Holy Spirit. That is why Saint Paul declares: "We do not know how to pray as we ought, but the Holy Spirit prays within us, crying 'Abba—Father.'" If we pray in mind and heart it is just to be in harmony with our deepest being as baptized, Christed persons. This is why we must pray—to be in harmony with who we really are. Not to be at odds with ourselves, but to be whole and integrated.

This, too, is why we must pray always. For our oneness with Christ is not a transitory thing, it is a permanent state. By baptism we have been radically remade in the image and likeness of the Only Begotten. We may viciously deface the likeness, but we can never remove the image. And it cries out to us to be true to who we are—to be true sons to the Father, and this is prayer.

We are prayer on the level of being. We want to be prayer on all the other levels. We are called to it by our own integrity. And we are called to it by the insistence of a divine lover. He comes from afar—the kingdom of heaven, but also from near, for God is everywhere. He crossed the boundaries of time and space—those relativities that so bind us. He plunged into the confinement of material components. He became human. He grew as we do. He walked our paths and spoke our words. And his message, in sum, is this: "I do not call you servants any longer…I have called you friends, because I have made known to you everything that I have heard from my Father" (John 15:15). We are invited into the inner life of the divine Trinity, to share in the inner communications of God. For this he prayed: "That they might be one, Father, as you in me and I in you—that they might be one in us."

To this we are called—to hear the inner secrets of God, to hear of a love beyond telling: "Even if a mother would forsake her child, yet I will never forsake you." "How I have longed to gather you as a mother hen gathers her chicks beneath her wings…." "My Beloved to me and I to my beloved…." "My secret is mine, my secret is mine." And to respond to it. This is prayer. And this is why we should pray. Divine goodness and love postulate it. Divine goodness expressed in our being calls for it. We cannot be true to who we are, we cannot be integral, if we do not pray, and pray without ceasing.

But why do *I* pray?

I do try to ground my life on these fundamental facts. I try to make space in my life to get in touch with them through reading and meditation, to let them surface and influence my way of living and my response to life. But in fact, more often than not, it is the feeling, the emotion of the moment, that impels my prayer. True, if there were not deep-seated convictions forming my basic attitude to life and all reality, my response to these emotions would not be prayer. There might be some native mysticism. There would be a lot of despair. But hardly true prayer.

But, because my life is grounded on these convictions, when I am touched by a beautiful spring day—such as today—my heart does sing to our Creator. Spring is here and all creation seems to be springing forth. The brown fields take on a hopeful green. The sunsets and sunrises stop me short—pinks and reds and golds, clouds so close they can be felt, gently inviting Marian blues. Nature caresses, impresses. Buds burst from dried and gnarled vines and branches. There is hope for us all. Tulips and daffodils shoot up too quickly to be believed and splotch their bright colors on the recently dark canvas. Birds sing. Spring is here. God is here. My heart sings—sings to him as I go about the daily task or wander down forest trails or sit at my window and write this. It was in the midst of sweaty toil, clearing the marshes of Clairvaux, that Saint Bernard was inspired to write:

> I have experienced it, believe me! You find God more in the forests than in the books. Woods and stones will tell you things you cannot hear from teachers.

But it is not only spring that makes me sing. Each season—and I am prejudiced enough to say, especially in New England, though I am sure it is true elsewhere; I have found it everywhere I have gone—has its beauty and its call as it speaks to us of the beauty, the love, and the care of the Creator. And our only response can be prayer—prayer of praise, of thanksgiving, of love to love.

Isaiah 11:2 spoke of our Lord:

> The spirit of the LORD shall rest on him,
> the spirit of wisdom and understanding,
> the spirit of counsel and might,
> the spirit of knowledge and the fear of the LORD.

Patristic tradition came to speak of these as the Gifts of the Holy Spirit, seven dispositions formed in our spirit at baptism and activated by the Holy Spirit, when and how and to the degree he wishes, though certainly in response to our longings and aspirations. It is by the gifts of knowledge and understanding and the action of the Holy Spirit that we readily perceive the presence of the Creator in his creation, that we understand—"stand under" and see what lies beneath the surface (the Latin word for understand is *intelligere*—literally, to read within). When the gift of wisdom is activated, we even "taste and see that the Lord is sweet" (the Latin word for wisdom—*sapientia*—comes from *sapor*—savor). It is the activity of these precious gifts—our desire for this activity and our openness to it—that transforms not only glorious spring days, but every day and every experience, into constant prayer.

It is not only beauty and presence that calls forth prayer from my heart. It is also pain and hurt and apparent absence. These are the dark days, and they can come even when the sun is shining and the birds are singing. The cloud that obscures all this may be a cloud indeed: sin or the struggle with temptation, real tragedy—personal or communal—or physical pain. Or it may be objectively some real trivia (which I will realize when the sun finally does break through) that wounds my pride, thwarts my will, frustrates the hope of the moment. It may be a tempest in a teapot, but for the moment all is dark and stormy and I am very threatened. I cry out, "Lord, save me, for I perish!" Why do I pray at such times? Because something deep within me repeats Peter's words: "Lord, to whom shall we go? You have the words of eternal life" (John 6:68). In my anguish, and sometimes it is indeed bitter anguish (I am sure you know what I mean, having felt it, too), I need help, love, presence, and even though it may be very dark and lonely, the Spirit yet speaks to my spirit in words beyond my hearing. In some deep way I know there is hope, there is reason to cry out. There is One there beyond the clouds who hears.

But I pray not only when the sun is shining or the clouds are pressing and depressing. I pray all the time, because I need to pray all the time. *Caritas Christi urget nos*—The love of Christ compels us. We are loved with an insatiable love and our own love is insatiable.

God is love, and we are made to the image of God. It is of our very nature to love. And to love without limit. For, being made in the likeness of God, we have been given hearts that have an infinite capacity for love. Nothing less than a deep intense complete love affair with God—total communion (and what else is prayer in its fullness?)—will satisfy us, fulfill us.

This is not only true of those who have embraced consecrated celibacy, although this has a special meaning in our lives: this is the meaning of our choice. We choose the celibate way to be fully free for this love. We choose celibacy because we choose Christ. I have to admit that the way celibacy was presented back in my seminary days made me conjure up the image of a man going to the altar thinking only of all the girls he was giving up instead of the girl he was about to marry. All the don'ts, the negativities of celibate life were stressed, but not the love affair with Christ. Celibacy for the kingdom is a positive choice to make Christ the love of our life. If this romance is not fostered and cultivated we celibates will be truncated human beings. We are all—all us humans—made for love. When the romance grows, prayer becomes not only an ontological necessity, but a deeply felt need. For prayer is nothing else but communication and communion with God. And we desperately need to communicate, to be one with our Beloved.

But this applies not only to celibates. Every human person has an infinite capacity and need for love. "You have made us for Yourself, O Lord, and our hearts will not rest until they rest in You." If married persons do not center their love in God, they cannot come to fullness even in their married love. This is undoubtedly one of the great causes of frustration in marriage—a frustration that leads to divorce, with the illusory hope that since this spouse did not fulfill me, I can find another who will. If spouses do not center their love in God, then they unconsciously expect their very finite partners to satisfy their infinite need for love. The result can only be frustration. But if a couple, married or engaged, or just special friends (and they can be of the same sex) center their love for each other in a shared love for God, then their mutual love is drawn up into this divine love and knows a fullness and completeness it can experience in no other way. This is why it is so important that lovers pray together and come to realize that their making love to each other is one of their greatest acts of prayer. I have heard of a couple who always have a candle lit before their picture of the Sacred Heart when they are making love—making love by candlelight, a light that sacramentalizes the divine dimension of their very human and fulfilling love. "The family that prays together, stays together" in more ways than one.

I could go on and on writing about this "why" of prayer. My whole life and yours is a "why" for prayer. The whole creation is, precisely because it is creation, a message of totally gratuitous love, love for us, to us. But do I really need to write anything at all? Let us just be still and *know* that he is God.

How Should
We Pray?

My first spiritual father, Dom Edmund, frequently admonished me, using the maxim of Dom Chapman: "Pray as you can, don't pray as you can't." What he was warning against was going to prayer with preconceived ideas, modeling our prayer on what we have read, on the prayer life and experience of this or that saint, of this or that friend or advisor. No! The prayer of each person is absolutely unique because it is a unique relation between the pray-er and our God of Love.

Saint Paul tells us quite frankly: "We do not know how to pray as we ought," adding: "but that very Spirit intercedes with sighs too deep for words" (Romans 8:26). This is certainly the bottom line in prayer. We do not know how to pray, how to give adequate expression to our relation with God, because we do not fully know ourselves as men and women who have been baptized into Christ and made partakers of the divine nature, and because we do not know God in any really adequate way. But the Spirit has been poured out in our hearts. He is Christ's Spirit. He is the bond of love, the pray-er who binds Father and Son and fully expresses their relationship. He can and does fully express, from the depths of our being, our relationship to the Father in the Son.

For our prayer to be in any way adequate, it must allow the Spirit to speak out within us. So we might conclude that the best prayer is that in which we are most silent, giving full freedom to the Spirit to express his prayer, his cry: Abba! Theoretically, maybe *yes;* practically, maybe *no.* More important than speaking or not speaking, than thinking or not thinking, is to will to have our will wholly in harmony with the will, the love, the movement of the Spirit—that is the important thing. If speaking, thinking, or imagining helps us at the moment to do this, we should by all means speak, think, use our imagination. But we must remember that prayer is supposed to be a communion, a communication, a dialogue between two lovers—not a monologue. And he, the Beloved, we must acknowledge, has a lot more to say that is worth listening to than we have. So we do need to make some effort at learning to listen. "Be still, and know that I am God!" (Psalm 46:10). Pondering on his words and actions, fleshing them out in our imagination, can be very helpful in getting us more involved in him, in calling forth our response and our love. But leaving ourselves open in longing love, inviting him to make his actual presence an experienced reality, will open the way to a much more complete communion.

If we have been blessed with the experience of a very beautiful and full love affair with another human person, we can perhaps learn something from it about the way to pray. We can recall that when we were first attracted to the other person, there was a great desire to be with that person. We had a lot to say. We wanted him or her to know all about us. We wanted to know all about our beloved. We needed the reassurance that our beloved wanted really to know us. As the relationship developed, speaking became less important. We wanted to be together, doing things together, getting to know each other more by the nonverbals, by the way the beloved acted and we interacted. The attraction grew; the desire for deeper and deeper communion grew. We wanted more and more just to be together, free from the distraction of speaking—words were so inadequate—and doing, just to be together, to melt into one. In the end we suffered the frustration of knowing that oneness with another can be attained only to a certain degree in this life, and together we looked with expectation to that life beyond where we would come into a oneness in God that would allow us to experience each other totally in a complete communion of being.

So, too, in our relationship with God. At first, a lot of talking. We have much to say. We want assurance that we are important to God. We tend to do a lot of asking, and expect a response that will affirm that he has heard us. But if the relationship is to grow it has to involve listening as well as speaking. Otherwise we will not hear his response—which may he quite different from what we expect. If we do not learn to listen, we may try to dictate what his response should be, and even conclude that he is not hearing us and not responding when he does not respond according to our dictates. So often this is the case when people speak of unanswered prayer. They did not hear his answer, because they were too busy with their own thoughts and words and were disposed to hear only one answer, the one they were projecting on God—and so they could not hear his true word of love to them.

At first it is not always easy to hear God. Our ear of faith, the ear of our heart, is not well tuned. The din of the world—the outer world and our own inner world—is too much with us. We need at this point, then, to make a good bit of use of the sacred

Scriptures, especially the gospels, where God reveals himself most fully in human form and speaks directly to us. "I do not call you servants any longer…I have called you friends, because I have made known to you everything that I have heard from my Father" (John 15:15).

Saint Teresa of Ávila, a great teacher of prayer, one whom the Lord drew into a most intimate and special kind of communion with himself, tells us that for years she could not pray unless she had the book of Scripture open before her. Some days we will listen to line after line of the Lord's words, and none will seem really to speak to us. On other days the first word may powerfully speak, make the Lord very present, and we will readily respond, in word, in thought, or in silent presence and communion, responding with our whole being.

This, then, is one way of praying: after coming into the divine presence and calling on the Spirit to help us (remembering those words of Saint Paul which we quoted above: "We do not know how to pray as we ought, but that very Spirit intercedes with sighs too deep for words," Romans 8:26), we read a passage of Scripture and begin to listen. As soon as the word of God speaks to us we stop, let it resonate within us, and respond in whatever way we are moved to do so. We may want to ask the Lord to help us understand more fully, to experience more deeply. We may want to begin to pour out our needs or those of others that we carry in our heart. We may want to think more on what we have read. We may just want to be with it, with him who has revealed himself in the word.

The advantage of this form of prayer is that it gives the Lord a chance to speak, and to speak, as it were, first, to open the conversation as he wishes. But some days we may indeed come to prayer with hearts too full. There is so much we need to say, or express in deeper ways. We may not need to hear through the Scriptures. He is present and that is enough for us. Let us pray as we can. But there will be days when he seems far away, when we feel no desire to speak to him or be with him. Then we will have to let him do most of the talking. We may even have to force ourselves, as it were, to be present to him and to listen. At such times we stop now and then to listen more intently, and then, perhaps painfully, go on as if his word were sterile, his presence an absence. The important thing is that we be there. "Speak, Lord, your servant wants to hear." Actually, our being there, our listening, is a response to his presence and activity. For if he were not present and acting, we would not be there. It is his grace that engenders our desire—even a cold, determined, willed desire to seek the apparently absent God.

He may speak now, and we hear him only later. Abbot Guerric of Igny, one of our twelfth-century Cistercian Fathers, has a very beautiful Easter sermon. In it he comments on the gospel scene where the three women encounter Christ on the garden path. They had gone to the tomb seeking him and found he was not there. They came away grieving, only to find him unexpectedly on the path as they went on their way. Guerric, inspired by this, reminds his sons:

> Many of you, if I am not mistaken, recognize what you have experienced, after Jesus, whom you sought at the altar, as at the tomb, and did not find, unexpectedly came to meet you in the way while you were working. Then you drew near and held on to his feet….What a consolation it will be also if he joins you as a companion on

the way and by the surpassing pleasure which his conversation gives, takes away from you all feeling of toil,
while he opens your mind to understand the Scriptures
which perhaps you sat and read at home without understanding.

I beseech you, my brethren, to whom God has on
occasion given the experience of this: was not your heart
burning in you on account of Jesus when he spoke to
you on the way and opened the Scriptures? Let them
then who have experienced it remember it and let them
sing in the ways of the Lord that great is the glory of the
Lord. Let those who have not experienced it, believe and
be eager to experience it... (Third Easter Sermon, 4).

At prayer we may sometimes feel as if we are at an empty
tomb, but it is important that we go on seeking, for "seek and
you shall find." But the finding may not be at the time of prayer.
It may be later when we are speaking to someone or quietly going about our business, walking down the street, driving the car,
waiting for the elevator....And suddenly, the Lord is very present,
the word comes alive, meaning is transformed.

We have seen how Saint Teresa used the Book to focus her
attention and elicit the presence. It may not always be possible,
or desirable, or most effective for us to do this. We have, traditionally, many other means. All creation can speak to us of God, for it
is a manifestation of him, every moment coming forth from him.
I have found God more in the trees and brooks than in the books,
said Saint Bernard. Byzantine Christians often pray before the
icons, which evoke a real presence. In the West, the tabernacle,
the host in the monstrance, have had a powerful attraction. We

have, too, our pictures and statues. The Stations of the Cross, with their fourteen tableaux, speak the word of love in image. Perhaps the favorite method of prayer among us is the rosary. While fingers on beads focus our attention and bring the body into prayer, the mind hears again the word of salvation, and with Mary's help and guidance, we respond to it. I saw in my own mother this simple form of prayer lead to that holiness which is a life of love lived for others.

In centering prayer it is a single, simple word, a meaningful word, a word of love, the name of the Beloved, that says all, and allows us to abide in presence and communion. Undoubtedly holy Communion itself calls us to the summit, when the divine host brings into our very being the message of love of Calvary, Cenacle, and Mass, and assimilates us in sacramental mystery.

I have often used this illustration: Suppose we have a very dear friend whom we meet every day at a coffee break. It becomes something important in our lives. If something comes up and prevents our meeting we really miss it. But, when we come together, we have not made any plans as to what we are going to say or what we are going to do. True, some days we go eagerly, bursting with some news, or burning with some question. But more often we simply go. We may not say much. Our friend may do most of the talking one day; we, another. And yet another day we may just sit and look out the window together. It is important to be together. After the coffee break we don't look back to ask ourselves what has happened—at least not ordinarily. We don't worry about what we said, how we communed. But we do come away refreshed, affirmed by love and presence, and our bond is a little stronger. We know we have someone we can depend upon, turn to, and call upon in need. We have a friend.

So prayer might be our coffee break with the Lord (and I wouldn't rule out a cup of coffee being part of our sitting down with the Lord—especially if it is early morning or we are afraid we might be overcome by sleep). Prayer is friendship in action—that high point of friendship when we are simply entering into and experiencing the reality that we and God are friends. What can be greater? What can more truly satisfy the deepest aspirations of our being? God and I are *friends*!

How do we pray? We pray as we can. And we don't want to get too introspective about it, making a project of it. It is simply spending time, communicating personally, intimately with someone we love. And doing it regularly.

Time Is of
the Essence

As I sat in my office this afternoon—surrounded by letters to be answered, phone calls coming in, books and papers to be read, galleys to be corrected, and plants to be tended—speaking with one of the young brothers who had come in for counseling, the first bell for Vespers warned us it was almost time for our evening prayer of thanksgiving. We quickly but peacefully concluded our session and started together for the church to join all our brothers in hymns and psalms and meditations.

It is easy for prayer (at least formal periods of prayer) to keep its due place in our lives when there are bells to remind us, supportive brothers to be with us, agreed times and places. It is not so easy when one is on his or her own. A personal rule of life can be a great assist. We will say more about this later. But even the best rule will not be of help if it is not undergirded by real convictions. And we do need to find support from fellow travelers.

Time is of the essence for prayer as long as we are wayfarers and our journey is through time. Indeed, we are to pray "always." But we will not pray "always" if we do not pray "sometimes." True, we should be able to say: "My work is my prayer." But we will not be able to say "My work is my prayer" if we do not have some prayer time. We won't know what prayer is, experientially speaking. We need time for prayer.

And this calls for making options. We have only a twenty-four-hour day. I have thought at times it would have been nice if God had given us a few more hours. But I have a hard enough time using those twenty-four hours consistently well, so I had better be quietly grateful for what I have. In these twenty-four hours I need to sleep, eat, and generally take care of my body, make time for friends, fulfill my duties towards others, get my work done, recreate, and, yes, make time for God—Mass, sacraments, reading, and prayer. How can it all fit in? It just doesn't. And so I have to make options—options that involve a great amount of pain. (What was it our Master said about taking up our daily cross? Did he, too, have to make options?)

Most of us, most of the time—some of us, all the time—find time for sleep and for food. Which is more important, the body or the soul? I am not suggesting neglecting the body. Indeed, we cannot hope to pray well if we do not take proper care of the temple, though we might need to reconsider just what proper care is. But we should have the same deep convictions about the need of the soul to be rested and nourished through prayer and prayerful reading. If on a particular day we are faced with a necessary choice, it might be well to forego some of the rest and nourishment of the body in order to respond to the needs of the soul.

In any case, we want to be profoundly convinced of the importance of making time each day to let ourselves rest in the Lord and be nourished by him. This is difficult for us. We are deeply formed by our society, which is wholly oriented to production.

Everything is evaluated by the measurable end product. And what do we get out of prayer? We know if we don't sleep, our productivity will suffer, so we are ready to "waste" time sleeping since we are convinced it is a necessary waste. But most of us have not prayed enough to experience how tremendously it heightens our productivity and how much productivity we are *de facto* losing by not praying. But even apart from this, we do need to waste time on God—on Life, on Love, on Friendship, in the truest sense.

One of my favorite gospel stories (I actually have quite a few favorites) is the beginning of John 12:1–8:

> Six days before the Passover Jesus came to Bethany, the home of Lazarus, whom he had raised from the dead. There they gave a dinner for him. Martha served, and Lazarus was one of those at the table with him. Mary took a pound of costly perfume made of pure nard, anointed Jesus' feet, and wiped them with her hair. The house was filled with the fragrance of the perfume. But Judas Iscariot, one of his disciples (the one who was about to betray him), said, "Why was this perfume not sold for three hundred denarii and the money given to the poor?" (He said this not because he cared about the poor, but because he was a thief; he kept the common purse and used to steal what was put into it.) Jesus said, "Leave her alone. She brought it so that she might keep it for the day of my burial. You always have the poor with you, but you do not always have me."

This text is a real scandal. Who is this man who so matter-of-factly declares "you always have the poor with you," and yet, while the poor go hungry, he condones thousands of dollars worth (three hundred days' wages) of exotic perfume being lavishly poured out to scent his body? What is he trying to say to us? What is his mentality? For we are counseled: "Let the mind be in you which was in Christ Jesus." In this instance we find ourselves more instinctively with Judas: "Why this waste?" The Lord is saying to us powerfully that even though human poverty will always have its terrible lonely needs, yet he wants us to pour out ourselves lavishly on him personally. Indeed, as Mother Teresa never got tired of saying, the ministry of the poor has no value if it is not ministry of Christ in them—their true dignity. And we will not serve or respond to Christ in the poor if we do not respond to him in himself.

When we stop in the middle of a busy day, with so many things to be done, so many brothers and sisters to be served, and sit down for a few quiet moments with the Lord, something deep in us cries: "Why this waste? Can't I be with the Lord in serving them?" Yes—but not for long if we do not spend some time with the Lord himself. Why? We can argue with some of the psychological reasons for this—the plain human reasons—but ultimately it is because he wants it so.

It is difficult for us to believe that God, the infinite God, really wants our time, our love, our attention, when we so often experience ourselves as so unlovable, so undesirable. And yet it is so. It is *the* reason why he created us. Anything we are able to do, he can easily get someone else to do—no doubt about it; anything, *but one thing*. There is one thing each one of us can do for God that no other person can ever do. And it is for this that he, as it were, dreamed through all eternity of bringing us into existence and now sustains us in existence. We alone can give him *our personal love.* It is for this he created us and keeps us in existence. He wants us to spend time loving him (just being with him in love), wasting time with him, pouring out our precious life's time on him.

Since I wrote that last line a good bit of time has elapsed. I could not but stop and enjoy for a while his presence, his love. Why don't you?

Now, let us get very practical. Stop for a bit and look over the past three days. Try to make a precise inventory of how you used those twenty-four hours which our God so graciously and gratuitously gave you. Are you happy about the way you spent that wealth?

Do you recall the day Jesus found himself in a desert place with thousands of people? They had been following him for days. The disciples gave voice to a very real concern. Food supplies had run out. It was time to send them home. Jesus was attentively compassionate. Well enough to send them home, but many stomachs were empty, and the journey was long....They must be fed....So he blessed the little that was on hand and all were fed. And then he gave the command: "Gather up the fragments" (John 6:12).

The Lord is lavishly generous to us with life and time, but he says to us, "Gather up the fragments." Looking over the last three days, what were the fragments? Did you really need to spend all that time in idle chatter, in perusing the whole newspaper, in dawdling over coffee, in daydreaming, in...?

Gathering up the "fragments" of your days, what do you have? Already there is a good bit of time you could spend in attending to the Lord, who dwells in the cell of your heart and at this very moment is bringing you forth in love and giving you the gift of life. Take these moments to plunge within—to thank, to ask, to embrace, to simply be with him. Use your own words or aspirations, or Scripture phrases that have meaning for you, or say nothing at all. Just be in the embrace of his affirming love for what moments you have. When the elevator arrives, when you reach your floor, when the day's doings call for your attention again, you will respond refreshed.

But does God, does such a benefactor, does such a loving Father, rate only the fragments of our life? He gives us all of life. Doesn't he rate a tithe? What do you think? To give God personally and directly one-tenth of the time he gives us seems little enough to me.

How do I see this? There is morning and evening prayer and grace at meals. There is the daily rosary. There is daily Mass and Communion, if we are fortunate enough to find Mass celebrated at a time that can fit into the demands of our state in life. To this I would add a fifteen- to twenty-minute period of meditation and at least ten minutes of *listening* to Jesus in the gospels twice daily.

I especially hope it is possible for you to attend Mass. It is a special contact with the summit of Christian reality. One fundamental truth we need to get a secure hold of: God is love. We are made to the image of God. Our life and our doings have meaning and worth only to the extent that they are expressions of love, and specifically of God's love.

We tend to see all things and times as sequential. One thing follows another. But that is not the way God sees things. God is in the eternal "now." All is present to him in its completeness. God is already enjoying you, as he always has, in all your ultimate beauty. The first time I realized this I was quite angry. Here I am, struggling along, and God is already enjoying the finished product, "Saint Basil." But then I thought of Matt Talbot, who for most of eighteen years lay drunk in the gutter before God raised him up and made him a saint. Things could be worse! God sees things, not sequential but rather—if we want to try to imagine it—all piled up in one mountain or heap. At the summit is the greatest act of love ever offered him from this creation, and everything else finds its place on that mountain to the extent to which it participates in that act of love. And that act of love is the act in which the greatest person who ever lived offered him the greatest thing in creation: the Son offering to the Father his human life, in love and obedience. At every moment we can in faith attach ourselves, our doings, to this supreme act of love. This is what we seek to do in a habitual way through our morning offering:

> O Jesus, through the Immaculate Heart of Mary, I offer you all my prayers, works, joys, and sufferings of this day, in union with the holy sacrifice of the Mass.

In the Mass the Lord left us, his Church, a ritual act by which we can plug into this supreme act of love: "Do this in memory of me." With the prayer and presence of the Church, our weak faith, which so often falters in keeping in touch with this love that makes all meaningful, can be intimately in touch with it, and be nourished by it for the day's journey. Mass is certainly something we want to try to have at the heart of our day.

But we will not be able to enter fully into the Mass if we do not devote other times to hone our faith. The ritual will quickly pass us by and the reality will elude us. This is why we need time to sit quietly at the Lord's feet—to listen to him speak to us through the gospels, to listen to him speaking to us in the intimacy of the depths, the center of our own being.

I have elsewhere written about formulating one's own rule of life. Let me review it here very briefly.

First, it is most important to be profoundly aware that we are more than human. We have been baptized into Christ. We have been made partakers of the divine nature. To be able to understand and appreciate ourselves we need God's help, we need the very Spirit of God. Read 1 Corinthians 2:9:

> "What no eye has seen, nor ear heard,
>   nor the human heart conceived,
> what God has prepared for those who love him"—
> these things God has revealed to us through the Spirit.

PRAY TO THE HOLY SPIRIT

Everyone has his or her definition of happiness. Mine is this: Happiness is knowing what you want, and knowing you have it or are on the way to getting it. The first thing we need to do is to decide what we want. So take a piece of paper and try to write down what you want…what you want in the long term: heaven, God, being with those you love, and so on. And on the short term: religion, vocation, marriage, work, joy, peace, health, and so on.

Now take a second sheet and write down what you need to

do or have in order to attain these goals. Be practical. How much sleep do you need each night to be human…and divine? Food, recreation, work, study, exercise…and prayer, Mass, sacraments, sacred reading…and at least some time of retreat each month to get in touch with yourself and reality.

Seeing all your needs, take a third sheet and look over the past few months. What has been preventing you from doing what you want, getting what you want? What in yourself, in your life, in others? Some practical plans as to what to do about these are called for.

And finally—and this is the difficult one—on a fourth sheet write up on a daily, weekly, and monthly basis a program for yourself. Why is this difficult? Because here we are back to the twenty-four-hour day. And we have to make options. If we are going to put first things first, some second things are going to have to be left behind.

Our schedule should include a monthly day of retreat, apartness. Husbands and wives might make this retreat together. Friends, too. But it would be well, at least at times, to go it alone. This will be a joy, not only because it will be a special time with the Lord—"I will lead him into the desert, and there I will speak to his heart"—but because we will see as we review our rule of life that our lives are going the way we want them to go, we are en route to attaining our heart's desire. And this is happiness.

Time is of the essence for those on a journey. Using it well to do what we want to do, to get what we want to get, is the key to happiness. If we want friendship with God—true, loving intimacy, which is what we are made for—then a significant amount of our time will be spent with him personally in prayer.

The Journey

Perhaps one of the greatest spiritual fathers the Christian community has ever known is Bernard of Clairvaux. Indeed, he seemed to father all of Christendom in the second decade of the twelfth century, the greatest of centuries before our own. Not only did his sons fill many of the episcopal sees, but in the last years of his life one of them sat on the seat of Peter. Kings and emperors looked to him as arbiter and counselor. But it was not only monks and clerics and the powerful of the earth that he touched. His letters are addressed to laypersons of every station and are filled with warmth and homey advice as well as lofty spiritual teaching. He is indeed all things to all insofar as this is humanly possible.

In 1136, Bernard of Clairvaux began publishing a series of sermons in the form of a commentary on the *Song of Songs*, a task he continued for seventeen years until his death in 1153. These sermons were eagerly awaited and quickly found their way to all parts of Europe, a marvel in itself considering the limited facilities of that age for publication and distribution. In the first twelve sermons, Bernard described in summary fashion the journey of the soul—a journey, for him, from the feet to the hands to the lips of our beloved Lord.

We begin at the Lord's feet. The Lord has two feet: justice

and mercy. Reflecting on his justice we are inspired with a certain fear, the beginning of wisdom, to turn from our sins. But the knowledge of his mercy keeps us from being overwhelmed by fear and gives us hope. Without such knowledge, without such hope, we might well despair, having nowhere to turn. But with such hope we turn to God. We reach up and kiss his hands.

His hands are liberality and strength. In response to our hope, he pours out his blessings. Grace and virtue grow in our lives and he strengthens us in our steadfast pursuit of him. Our experience of this goodness fills us with gratitude. We steadfastly seek more and more the author of all this good, the Lord himself. We seek union with him, the kiss of his mouth.

The "kiss" of God is the Holy Spirit, the total expression of the love of the Father and the Son. And it is the Spirit of Love who is now poured out into our hearts, uniting us intimately, not only with himself, but with the Father and the Son. He comes to "teach us all things" through activating those gifts we have all received at baptism. He brings us into that kind of knowledge of God, which comes only from being united to him in love: love-knowledge.

This union with God cannot but be fruitful. It makes us like unto God, a Father compassionate and confirming. Like the Son, we take to ourselves in compassion all the misery and needs of all our brothers and sisters and do what we can to relieve them, even as we congratulate them, affirming all their goodness. For Bernard, the gift of contemplative union—the union that comes about from knowing God intimately through love—is never given solely for the benefit of the recipient, but for him or her as a member of a community and of the body of the Church. It implies a share in God's own compassionate, creative goodness.

The journey, then, is a simple one, though it may not be so quick and easy. And we, indeed, may make it a very long and complicated one by our lack of simplicity. Maybe a few pointers can be helpful:

1. First of all, we need to avoid looking at this journey as though it were a sort of ladder, one step to be mounted after another, and the lower rung left fully behind as we mount to the higher. It is true that the image of the ladder is a favorite one, frequently used by the Fathers, drawing on biblical imagery. But if we must see this as a ladder, let us see it as a ladder lying flat on the ground, so that we can walk on all the rungs at the same time. For, in fact, while the graces of one state may well dominate at a particular period in our life, there is nothing to prevent the Lord from offering other graces at the same time—and he often does. No matter what stage of spiritual growth we have attained, in this journey we can never leave behind a due fear of the Lord and of our own weakness, nor hope, gratitude, longing, and perseverance. Each has its place.

2. We want to watch over our dispositions and be ever mindful that the Lord does have two feet. If we find ourselves inclined to be depressed, worrisome, cast down, it is time for us to dwell more fully on the foot of mercy. We do well to listen to the loving words of our Savior, especially the parables of divine prodigality and the outpourings of the Sacred Heart at the Last Supper. However, if we find we are being slack in our practice, careless about temptations, sin, and infidelities, then it is time to reach for the foot of justice. Let us listen to the sterner warnings of the Lord. It is well for us to make a list for ourselves of these passages of the gospels and other books of the Bible that have most powerfully

and effectively spoken to us of his justice and of his mercy, so that we can return to them according to our need.

3. Let us always give thanks. The daily prayer of the Church always includes Mary's *Magnificat,* inviting us, with her, to glorify him who has done great things for us. Holy is his name. His mercy is from generation to generation. Thanksgiving keeps us looking at the fullness of reality. It keeps us positive and hopeful. I often say that the world is made up of two kinds of people: those who look at the doughnut and those who look at the hole. Sin and evil are but a lack of due good. It is always resident in a good. No matter how evil the actions of a man may be, he retains his essential being, a likeness to God, a goodness capable of all good. And this we can celebrate in thanksgiving and hope. Thanksgiving fills us with hope and points us ever upward, keeps us ever expectant, and, because he said: "Seek and you shall find," it makes us the recipient of ever greater gifts.

4. In the course of tracing out our own journey, Bernard makes a magnificent point. Let me quote a passage:

> Many of you, as I remember in the manifestations of conscience which you make to me privately, are wont to complain of this aridity and langour of soul, this heaviness and dullness of mind, whereby you are rendered incapable of penetrating the profound and hidden things of God and can experience little or none of the sweetness of this spirit. What is that, my brethren, but a longing to be kissed?

What Bernard is saying here is very important, and should be very consoling to many pray-ers. He is pointing out the fact that when we have made progress in the spiritual journey, there comes a time when we begin to so perceive this divine goodness that the gifts of God no longer satisfy. We want God himself. The result is a sense of dryness, deprivation. The spiritual lights, the sense of progress that formerly delighted us, mean nothing now. We want something more, something other, Someone Other. Thus dryness, a sense of dullness, an awareness that the prayers and practices of the past, perhaps even the sacraments, do not attract us and call forth our devotion and is not a sign we are falling back. Quite the contrary. This indicates we have progressed to the point of a certain purity of heart and aspiration that can be drawn and satisfied only by God himself.

5. There is a danger inherent in reflecting on the spiritual journey. The all-too-human desire to make progress can take over. We can become more concerned about the journey, about how we are doing, than with the end. But the only way we can actually hope to make progress on the journey is to keep our eyes on the end, to truly seek God. The quest for virtue, for progress, or even for a deeper prayer can devolve into self-seeking, self-satisfaction, unless they are sought solely for the sake of God, as a means of attaining to him. Yet it is valuable to know our way, to know how best to make progress. Otherwise we will just stumble along and perhaps even impede our own progress. But we must not mistake means for end, or get too caught up in the means. We want to use them freely and wisely, but ever keep the eyes of our attention, of our heart, fixed on our goal, on our God.

One of the best helps we can find to do this is a good spiritual guide. I have often heard people say it is very difficult to find a spiritual guide. I wonder though if what was said by an abbot I know isn't nearer the truth: The problem is not the shortage of spiritual fathers and mothers, but of those who really want to be open and receive guidance. We fear the exposure. And we fear a fallible guide will ask things of us we are not, or should not, or do not want to do. For spiritual guidance we do not need a John of the Cross or a Teresa of Ávila. The Holy Spirit is really the only true director. What we need is someone who will walk with us on the journey and help us listen to the Spirit. If the brother or sister has a lot of learning, good; and a lot of experience, better, provided these do not stand in the way of true humility.

What are the qualities we want in the person to whom we turn for spiritual guidance?

- First of all, we want a person of prayer, one who will pray for us and with us, in our quest to know clearly the will of God and to live it.
- Second, we want a humble person (I am not listing these qualities in order of importance) who knows his or her own sin and weakness and, therefore, can be compassionate and understanding.
- Third, we want a good listener; someone who knows how to listen to God, who can help us to learn how to do that and can really listen to us.
- Fourth, then, we want a person with whom we feel we can, at least in time, share everything, even those deep secrets we are almost afraid to share with ourselves. Many of us have the experience of thinking: If people knew this or that about me, they would never love me or accept me. Fewer of us have had the experience of getting out such a fact and discovering that it really did not make

that much difference, or perhaps even made the confidant love us all the more. Misery loves company. And Jesus, our God and our Savior, came for the miserable. Complete openness with another human is a very liberating and empowering experience.

- Fifth, we want a person with enough prudence to advise us to see an "expert" when and if special questions or needs arise that demand expert guidance. For most of us, that is fairly rare. We just need to be faithful in following our own little way.

- Finally, we want as our guide or companion on the way someone who will love us, love us enough to pray for us, give us time, encourage us and affirm us, and, when we need it, give us a good kick in the rear—all with our permission, of course.

Such a person is really not that hard to find. Reflect for a moment. Couldn't you yourself do that for someone else? And wouldn't you, if asked? I am sure you would. And you would feel good for being asked, privileged to be asked to so share life with another. Perhaps, in God's design, another is waiting for you to call him or her forth by asking that she or he walk intimately with you on life's journey.

When we think of spiritual guidance, we do tend to think of priests, and perhaps today, also of nuns. (Note: I have been avoiding the more common term "spiritual direction." I believe only one can direct us, the Holy Spirit of God, who has become by baptism our Spirit. Others are to help us tune into that direction.) Certainly, there is a benefit when our guide is a priest and can bring the healing grace of the sacrament of reconciliation to the wounded areas we look at together. But there is obviously no reason why we cannot bring them to a priest for sacramental ministration after we have looked at them with our guide and friend. Any fellow Christian who has the qualities outlined above and who is willing to walk with us in faith can be a sacrament of God's presence and an instrument of his grace. In response to the faith and trust, the humility and purity of heart we express in asking one to serve us in this way, the Lord will respond. He will be present when we two meet in his name.

Right in the beginning, our Creator said, "It is not good that man [or woman] should be alone" (Genesis 2:18). We should courageously and confidently choose a companion for the journey. We will quickly find, it will be a journey to Emmaus. A third will join us and our hearts will begin to burn. And in the end our eyes will be opened and we will enjoy a successful journey and communion with our Lord.

In the Desert—
Dryness

Most men and women who seek a serious relationship with God in prayer come, sooner or later, to speak of "dryness" in prayer—the desert. They have known periods of fervor when everything in them united to pray and when they really enjoyed prayer. God seemed very present, or at least they felt he could be easily reached. But such a gift—and such devotion is a gift— does not always last. If it is lasting in your case, certainly, do not feel guilty about it or feel as if you are missing something. Rejoice in the gift and use it to the full. God leads each one in the way he knows is best for that person. Some are led always in the light, in the way of sweetness and attraction. They can never have enough time for prayer. This is the source of their suffering. But they have to take care to keep a pure heart. We are, as my spiritual father used to remind me, to seek the God of consolation and not the consolation of God. To seek good feelings and emotions, the consolations of prayer, for ourselves would be to use God in some way; it would be still seeking ourselves and our own satisfaction, instead of seeking God.

For most of us, though, periods of fervor and sensible devotion are interspersed with times of "dryness," when God seems quite absent, or very far away, and we experience no strong inner compulsion to pray. This, too, of course, is God's gift. If God were simply absent from our lives we would not sense the lack. We would be as so many who are caught up in the things of this world. They go along completely oblivious of God, quite content with their worldly pursuits, conceiving of no other alternative, until one day, in his mercy, God breaks into their lives in one way or another. We experience God's apparent absence or distance precisely because he is present, touching the deepest part of our being, giving it that taste which makes it hunger all the more. "Everyone who drinks of this water will be thirsty again" (John 4:13).

You may say: "This is not quite how I experience it. I know I should pray, but I feel no desire to pray. In fact I feel a real repugnance; trying to communicate with someone who just isn't there or who seems to ignore me completely is too painful." But again, I say, you would not sense him as ignoring you if you did not sense his presence; you would not sense an absence if you did not know an existence, and all of this would not be painful if something deep in you did not tell you that communion with him is vital to your happiness. And all of this is a grace and a presence of God in your life.

"Dryness," then, should not be looked upon as something bad or undesirable. It is good. It is God's gift to us, the grace of the moment, precisely the grace we need at the moment. He challenges us and purifies us. Actually, if we are going to pray solely to give ourselves to God and let him bring about in us what he wants, then we always have what we want in prayer—dryness or consolation, it makes no difference—and we are deeply happy. But our hearts are not all that pure. There is a lot of self-seeking, even in our prayer. We do tend to look for consolation in our prayer, or at least some sign that we are really pleasing God and getting closer to him in some way. We are, in a word, seeking something for ourselves, rather than being pure gift, simply giving ourselves to God in love. It is for this reason dryness is painful. And it is precisely for this reason we need to experience periods of dryness, so that we will realize our self-seeking and let go of it, so that we will learn how to simply give ourselves in love without seeking any return, without seeking assurance, giving ourselves in confident, joyful love. As Saint Teresa has put it, we should serve the Lord as grandees, conscious of the privilege of waiting on him, rather than as servants working for a reward.

So, dryness is a time of grace. But how do we respond to such a grace? Certainly, there is the temptation to run away from it, to seek some salve for the pain, some consolation, to give up seeking an absent God, either by making him present in some way of our own or to just stop seeking.

Fidelity is extremely important here. We should have our basic rule of life, for good times and bad. And when we are dry and in the desert we should be especially faithful to it, going to our meeting place with the Lord, and being there even when he seems to fail to keep the appointment. Saint Teresa shares with us how for years she went to prayer, a book in hand, waiting in aridity for her Lord to readmit her to his fond embrace. Not even the words of the book could speak to her, because her soul longed for a deeper communication. We go to our time of prayer simply to give ourselves to the Lord and to wait on him, our love being great enough to say: "Not my will, but thine be done. Be it done unto me according to your will." If he wants to come with consolations or illuminations—wonderful. If he wants to leave us sitting there—fine. As he likes. We may want to use a book, especially the gospels, to keep ourselves focused, attentively present, longing; or maybe an icon. Or, more simply and more interiorly, a prayer word, as we do in centering prayer.

What we want to be careful of, though, is not to be seeking to escape the pain of the "absence" of God by conjuring up our own images of God and generating our own feelings. It certainly is quite legitimate to listen eagerly to his words of love in the gospels. And these might, indeed, evoke a response on various levels. But it is quite possible that at this time they will not, because the Lord wants to communicate with us at a deeper level and does not want us to be distracted by thoughts, images, or feelings on the more superficial level. "I will lead her into the desert and there I will speak to her heart." We want to "be still and know that he is God."

Fidelity, then, is very important during the season of dryness, the time in the desert, trusting in him to provide the manna and the theophanies as we need them. But, while fidelity is basic, it is not enough. Or rather, just being faithful to putting in our time at prayer is not enough. We must be faithful in truly seeking God, be faithful in expecting much from him. Yes, we are puppies under the table who should be grateful for the crumbs. But we are also, by his great mercy, sons and daughters seated at the table. We are friends. "I do not call you servants any longer …but I have called you friends" (John 15:15). We are the spouse of the Song of Songs, invited to the most intimate embrace. Our faithful coming to prayer should also be a faithful asking and seeking forevermore fullness in our union and communion with him and with him in his work of universal salvation. We should not seek to fill the emptiness with a lot of mental activity that may well prevent us from hearing the "still small voice," but we should fill it with intense longing and seeking. Our dryness, which brings home to us our unworthiness, our sinfulness, our impurity, our weakness, should not result in our being content with crumbs, however savory. Rather, confident in God's mercy, we should dare and seek all the more. I believe our greatest sin is that we expect too little of and for ourselves, because we expect too little of God. Having less, we expect more, because he is merciful love.

This indicates what our response to dryness should be outside the time of actual prayer. Saint Bernard, in the first sermon he preached on the Song of Songs, tells us that God has two feet: one of justice and one of mercy. He says that at times he clung too long to the foot of mercy and tended to become lax. Then he had to shift over to the foot of justice. But if he clung too long to this foot he would soon begin to despair. In time of dryness we need to cling more to the foot of mercy. In our reading we should listen with open ears and heart to the outpourings of the Sacred Heart, especially in the Last Supper discourse and the parables of mercy, listen to the chosen apostle, Paul, and to the exciting and provocative poetry of the Song of Songs. We can also turn to others—to the Fathers, or the spiritual writers of today, to anyone who will help engender in us a greater desire for the Lord.

In a time of real desert experience, all of this may seem like so much grist for the mill, producing only chaff. Yet, here again, fidelity is important. Faith comes through hearing. We listen to the word, awaiting the visit of the Word. And these words that perhaps don't seem to speak now do flow over the soul, purifying, deepening the grooves of love and desire, which will help us to be true in faithful longing during times of prayer. Sometimes the Lord speaks by silence. We are taken beyond the seemingly incomprehensible *koan* to the reality where what words could not communicate is spoken in our hearts in that language which the heart alone understands.

It is important while we are in the desert, in a season of dryness, that we keep close to our spiritual father or guide and to our friends. One can easily get lost in the desert. We need the guidance of one who has gone this way before and knows the route, one who can assure us that our steps are right and that the goal we seek is at the end. And we need our companions for the journey. The drab sameness of the terrain belies our progress. We can easily become discouraged. But friends who share our conviction of the value and the rightness of the journey will lighten the burden and help to make the time pass quickly as they share with us in love, joy, and hope.

We can indeed be tempted to look back, if not to the flesh pots of worldliness and the bondage of sin, at least to the security and consolations of the prayers of our youth. But it is through the desert that we come to the Promised Land, even in some ways in this life; and the desert has its own graces. We are fed with bread from heaven and are allowed to drink from the Rock who is Christ. There are special theophanies, manifestations of God's love and care; he enables us during this desert journey to overcome many of our enemies. If we have complete confidence in him it can be a relatively short journey, but, short or long, if we are faithful it will bring us to that purity of heart and clarity of vision where we will truly see God and find love, peace, joy—all the fruits of the Spirit.

Those Darn Distractions—
Bless Them!

If you ask friends who have been faithful in prayer what has
been their greatest challenge, if they don't answer "dryness,"
they will most surely say "distractions." For many pray-ers, distractions are public enemy number one. If that is so for you, I
would like to invite you to change your outlook and see them in
another light.

First of all, we can see the distraction precisely as a challenge, the sort of challenge our Lord gave voice to when he asked
Peter: "Simon son of John, do you love me more than these?"
(John 21:15). Each time we are at prayer, and the thought or
image of some person or thing grabs our attention, we can, as it
were, hear our beloved saying to us: "Do you love me more than
this person, more than this thing?" And we can respond very
concretely by turning our attention from the intruding person
or thing, fully back to the Lord. It is an affirmation of preferen-
tial love. So we can then look upon each distraction as a grace, an
invitation from the Lord, to renew and intensify our choice of
him over everyone and everything else.

But there is another way of looking at the intrusion. Again,
as an invitation from the Lord, but this time as an invitation to

consecrate to him the person or thing and our relation with that person or thing. We can lift him or her or it up to God in prayer and ask him to purify our hearts in regard to this concern, this love, this worry, this hope. The distraction then becomes an occasion for prayer, for sharing our concern with our beloved, for letting go of our care: "Cast your cares upon the Lord, for he has care for you." Anything that concerns us concerns our Lord also, no matter how trivial or how mundane it may seem. *Son, they have no wine.*

The distraction, too, invites us to a bit of self-examination and perhaps a step toward greater purity of heart. *Why*, we might ask ourselves, *do thoughts of this person or these things have the ability to pull me away from attention to the Lord? Is my relationship here all that it should be? Is this relationship centered in the Lord?* We may perceive an invitation or admonition to greater detachment or to relinquishing something that shackles us in our Godward journey.

So, then, it is sometimes good just to turn back to the Lord, away from the distraction, renewing the attentiveness of our love, using the distraction as an opportunity to intensify that love. At other times we may draw the distraction into our prayer and make it the matter of our conversation with the Lord. On other occasions we may see in the distraction an invitation to examine ourselves before the Lord in order to grow in purity of heart. In all such cases, the distraction becomes a grace. And like every grace, if we respond to it the way the Lord wants us to, it becomes an occasion of growth.

But what about community prayer—the Mass or the Office? Here the Church is praying, and we are praying with her. We are not free to go off on our own tangents. Or are we? In the

West we do tend to expect all to be attentive to this one prayer when we gather together in community. But this is not so in all authentic Christian traditions. In the Eastern rite it is quite common and most acceptable for a small group to be chanting the psalms, let us say, while the priests are saying other prayers before the altar or at the preparation table, and for many of the devout to be quietly in their places saying the Jesus Prayer or standing before an icon communing with a favorite saint. We have had something similar to this in the West in May or October devotions, when the people recited the rosary while the priest said the prayers of the Mass. This is frowned upon now, and perhaps rightly so. But we should not adopt too univocal an idea of community prayer and allow for communion in the depths.

In any case, when one is actually saying a particular prayer, it is desirable that the mind be one with the voice. When we are reciting some prayer alone, we can leave off the recitation and follow the invitation of the distraction. But when we are in community we do not have the same freedom. What, then, are we to do?

First of all, let us peacefully be aware of our basic option. We are at community prayer precisely because we do want to pray. We want to speak to the Lord and have him speak to us through the Scriptures and the prayers of the Church. We do not want this distraction or we could have stayed at home and enjoyed it to the full.

The basic being to God, which is what truly constitutes the prayer, continues in spite of the unwanted vagaries of the mind. We need not fret, then, but simply return to the Lord when we become aware of what is going on. This is not the time to get all upset with ourselves, or to engage in acts of repentance. This will only keep us away from what we are supposed to be about. We can do our repenting and penancing later, if we will. For now we gently return to the prayer of our lips, so that heart and mind are one with voice unto the Lord.

Outside the time of this formal community prayer we might well do something about our distraction, besides the repentance already mentioned. We might ask the Lord to deliver us from distractions, to give us more fervor and devotion, if he sees that this is best for us. We can prepare for our prayer. Spiritual reading can stir up our fervor. Study of the psalms and the Mass texts can better dispose us to stay with them. As the time of prayer approaches, we can consciously lay aside engaging concerns and seek to free ourselves from them. We can very consciously sign ourselves with holy water, renewing our baptismal commitment and our awareness of the indwelling Trinity. It is said of Saint Stephen Harding that as he dipped his fingers in the font he left all his concerns there and entered the church completely free. We could try the same. Very consciously we can come into the divine presence. Saint Benedict says that whenever we undertake any good work, we should first most insistently ask for the divine help to bring it to perfection. Traditionally the Church begins her prayer with this cry: "O God, come to my assistance. O Lord, make haste to help me." If we do all this, we have done our part. The rest is up to the Lord. Remember, of ourselves we can accomplish no good. All good comes from him. If he wants us to be attentive at prayer in a unified way on all levels, that is his business. He must bring it about. And if he doesn't, we have to accept our poor distracted state, humbly and peacefully, knowing that this is the will of the Lord for us now. This does not detract from the reality, and, in God's eyes, the beauty of the prayer, so long as our will to pray, to commune with him, remains.

But what about contemplative prayer, where we are drawn to abide silently, lovingly, in the divine presence, in the divine embrace? Strictly speaking, there is no such thing as distractions in contemplative prayer.

In active prayer or discursive meditation we use thoughts and images as part of our prayer. Thus other thoughts and images do take us away from our prayer, distract us, and they have to be let go or integrated into the prayer. But contemplative prayer is at a different level. In itself it does not involve thought or image. It is at the level of will, love, being. While we rest in the depths in the movement and embrace of love, the thoughts and images continue to flow at their own level, in no way impeding our prayers, except when we let them draw us up to their more superficial level. If this happens before we are aware of it, no harm done. As soon as we are aware, we just simply sink back into the current of love and let the thoughts flow on their own level.

Saint Teresa of Ávila has a good image for this. When she was an elderly woman she was hurrying about Spain, busy doing the thing women do best: reforming the men. One day she described her experience in this way: "My life seems to flow along, as it were, in two great rivers, the one flowing into all these activities and the other flowing into God. But these two rivers are one." I think this is a very good image. Our lives are a great river, flowing out from the overflowing creative love of God and flowing on into the ocean of his love. Because we are men and women of love, this deep steady current of our lives is a flow of love into God. But on the surface we have many things: busy little tug boats, heavily laden freighters, pleasure yachts, garbage scows, pollution—

we have it all! In contemplative prayer we sink down into the deep current of love, leaving all the surface traffic behind. And it just flows along on its own while we flow into God in love.

I think we all have moments when we fantasize: If I were God, I would have made things different—better! One of my fantasies was this: If I had made man I would have put in a few good turnoff switches, so that when I went to prayer I could turn off thoughts, turn off memory, turn off imagination, turn off hearing—then what wonderful, deep, peaceful prayer I could have! But God is wiser than I (to say the very, very least). He has other plans.

Our Lord said: "Come to me, all you that are weary and are carrying heavy burdens, and I will give you rest" (Matthew 11:28). Prayer is supposed to be refreshing. (It certainly won't be if we spend our prayer time battling with distractions. This is why it is important to learn now to use distractions positively, in active prayer, and to learn that there is no such thing as distractions in contemplative prayer, but only thoughts that God wants to use.) If we relax properly and compose our bodies before prayer we will be physically refreshed at the end. Our spirits should be refreshed from our spending time with our beloved, experiencing his great love for us. And our minds and our whole psychological makeup is refreshed by the flow of thoughts and images. But we must let them flow freely while we attend to the Lord. If we try to control them or stop them, we will only build up tension and be exhausted at the end of the prayer instead of being refreshed. We will have spent the time trying to achieve some kind of state in ourselves (thoughtlessness, mindlessness—maybe a form of quietism) instead of being to and with the Lord.

This is perhaps one of the most difficult aspects of the transition from active prayer to a deeper, more contemplative prayer. In active prayer, intruding thoughts are distractions. While I have made a plea above for not considering them bad or enemies of our prayer, but as something we can use positively, nonetheless they are something we have to do something about. Not so in contemplative prayer. In this prayer we have to realize that thoughts and images are good in themselves, and God has a purpose for them to refresh us on the psychological level. But we have to let the Lord use them the way he wants to, and just let them flow as we rest in the Lord in the deepest level of our being, at the center where we are coming forth from his constantly creative love.

Distractions—thoughts and images, sounds and feelings—may well remain the number one challenge to our prayer, but they are not enemies. They are rather a challenge that can lead to a fuller, richer, more refreshing prayer. So those darn distractions, bless them, and thank God for them as gifts from him, calls to something more, the more we so much want.

Making Intercession

Recently a freelance writer came to the abbey to interview me. Her first question was a very typical one: "Coming from the heart of the city, a city which like any other is so filled with human misery, with crime and violence, with the lonely, the sick, and the aged, to this seeming paradise amid the hills," the writer demanded, "how can you, as a committed Christian, stay here doing nothing when there is such crying need outside?"

There came to my mind a rather humorous incident from the life of Thomas Merton, Father Louis of Gethsemane Abbey. It was back in the early 1960s. Professor Glen Hinson of the Southern Seminary took a class of his students out to the abbey for a visit—a rather unusual, indeed courageous, thing for a Southern Baptist to do in those almost preecumenical days. Father Louis was assigned to receive the visitors and show them around the monastery. Of course, the name and the person were unknown to these "separated brethren." At the conclusion of the tour of the buildings, and the explanation of the life, during which there had been many questions, one of the students asked Merton: "What's a smart guy like you doing holed up in a place like this?" Father Louis' answer was simple and powerful: "I believe in the power of intercessory prayer."

"Ask, and it will be given you" (Matthew 7:7). The Lord's

word is simple and straightforward. "If you have faith the size of a mustard seed, you will say to this mountain, 'Move from here to there,' and it will move" (Matthew 17:20).

This teaching of our master is repeated again and again by his disciples. John, the beloved one, tells us in his first epistle: "Knowing that whatever we ask, he hears us, we know that we have already been granted what we asked of him." Saint James, using imagery that we can quickly catch hold of, stresses the importance of faith on our part: "But ask in faith, never doubting, for the one who doubts is like a wave of the sea driven and tossed by the wind; for the doubter, being double-minded and unstable in every way, must not expect to receive anything from the Lord" (James 1:6–7). We have experienced the counter forces of pounding surf and treacherous undertow both on the ocean shore and in our prayer.

Thus, there are two challenges in intercessory prayer: first, believing in its power, and second, giving it its due place in our lives.

How can we increase our belief in the power of prayer? First of all, we can pray. Like the anguished father who so longed for the cure for his child, we too can cry out. "I believe; help my unbelief!" (Mark 9:24). We know the longing to be healed, to be touched, to be consoled, comforted, forgiven, to have a savior. Yet we experience the undertow of doubt. We can only cry out, asking the Lord to channel our forces on every level into a steady stream of faith and confidence.

We can assist and strengthen this prayer by Scripture meditation. The sacred text is filled with examples of prayer being heard, oftentimes in miraculous ways. In response to needs, great and small, God, sometimes feigning reluctance, reaches out and generously fulfills.

One example of this that rather delights me is the "first sign" that took place at Cana in Galilee. Mary had been invited to a wedding. And also, her son. But he showed up with a newly acquired band of croonies. These hearty fishermen may well have been a big part of the problem, but long before the festivities were due to end, the beverage supply was coming to an end. Mary, the watchful, the compassionate, became aware of the embarrassing situation that was arising before it was generally noted. She could think of only one solution quick enough to meet the need. As she turned to her son, she was greeted with a rather enigmatic response. Many interpretations have been laid upon it, but I think one thing is obvious. Jesus is a bit uncomfortable with the request. "After all, Mother, do you want it to go down in sacred history that the first miracle worked by the Son of God on earth was to turn out more booze for the boys after they had drunk the house dry?" We know Mary's response. And we know Jesus'. The boys got their booze.

But Mary is the mother of God, the All Sinless One. Let us turn to another model with whom we can all more readily identify, dear ole Saint Peter—not yet a saint and so delightfully capable of putting his foot in his mouth. It had been quite a day …and night. First, there was the shattering news of the beheading of John—in itself bad enough, but made more heartsickening by the revolting circumstances: a tip for a lustful dance. Ugh! The desire to go apart and grieve for a while, a very human and real need. Then the pressing crowds, the magnificent teaching, and the exciting and wondrous banquet, not from heaven but from their own fishermen's gnarled hands. And now the long hard night. A lot to think about as backs bent against the wind and pulled hard on the oars. And then suddenly he was there, a few yards away, gracefully walking along as though the surging sea were a rolling field. "'Lord, if it is you, command me to come to you on the water.' He said, 'Come!'" And impetuous Peter, who impetuously asked a miracle, impetuously leaped out of the boat and started running toward the Lord whom he really loved and trusted. But before his dash was ended, it came home to him what he had so impetuously done. He, Peter, the experienced fisherman, knew that things like this just did not happen. He had jumped or fallen into the sea too often. The undertow of reason dragged back the surge of faith. He began to sink. But all was not lost. There was still enough faith to cry out: "Lord, save me!" "You of little faith, why did you doubt?" (Matthew 14:31). The Lord reached out and the two safely walked back to the boat and climbed in. "Ask, and it will be given you" (Matthew 7:7).

But how, we might ask, can my prayer change things? Isn't the course of history largely set? Doesn't God already know what is going to happen? I do not think this is the place to consider at length the mysterious interrelation of God's foreknowledge and our freedom. Suffice it to say that in his eternal "now" God knows all that will occur in our unfolding time and the way one thing will affect another. He knows what will happen and what will happen because of our prayer.

One thing we do want to get hold of, though, is this reality: God's creating is constant. He does not just make things, persons, and then set them down and walk away. Ultimately there is one: God. Everything and everyone else exists by sharing in some way in his being. At every moment God is bringing forth and sustaining us in being, sharing with us his being. This is true for us, his images, his noblest creatures, and all else. Now, he has willed that what he brings forth and the way in which he brings things and persons forth in each moment will in part be determined by our prayer. This is the source of the power of our prayer, and it invests it with the power of God. "Ask, and it will be given you" (Matthew 7:7).

This being so, can we exaggerate the importance of our prayer and of praying constantly? We still stand on the brink of nuclear holocaust. At any moment there could be, by chance or by malice, an eruption that could mark the end of human life on our planet, if not the end of the planet itself. Our prayer can forestall the folly or failure that can unleash such an armageddon. At each moment sinners are coming, slowly or abruptly, to the end of their lives and are face to face with judgment. Our prayer can obtain for them the grace of conversion that they may die turned towards our God of love and his gift of eternal life. At every moment, famine stalks our world, armed conflict maliciously destroys life and its environment, natural disasters are taking their toll, and the horrors of prison camps and other forms of internment degrade human existence. Our prayer can eliminate all this. *If we believe,* and without wavering, send our prayerful concern to the heart of God.

This, we have to humbly confess, is probably the principal reason why in fact our prayers accomplish so little. We do waver in our hearts, we do not believe much in their power. As we have said, we need to pray for that faith: "I believe; help my unbelief!" (Mark 9:24). And we need to buoy up our faith by sacred reading.

But what, you might ask, if two or more ask for different outcomes? Devout Germans probably prayed for a German victory in World War II; certainly Americans were praying for an American victory. Cannot God's answer to prayer be "No!"?

God will give us whatever we want, asking in prayer, what

we truly want, not what we say we want or even think we want. God listens to the heart, not to the lips. He knows, too, how limited is our understanding and knowledge. He sees our truest desires and knows how they can best be fulfilled. And this is what he grants. We may not see it at the moment, but we will in time. The Germans prayed for victory, because they believed this could best lead to prosperity and peace. Actually the termination of the Nazi regime and Allied help to rebuild the nation were to prove more conducive to this.

To give a more homey example. Recently at dinner my three-year-old nephew laid eyes on the big shining carving knife and wanted it to play with it. He got a definite "No" from his loving parents. He could not see why they were so mean. Their loving care was not evident to him. But what he was really seeking, his happiness—to be found, he thought, in playing with that big shining knife—was best served by the parental "No." If God seems to be saying "No" to some prayers, it is because he is saying "Yes" to the deepest prayer of our hearts.

This realization, that the prayer God hears is the deep concerns of our hearts, answers another question. Realizing the importance and power of our prayer and wanting to respond to the evangelical precept to pray always, we ask: How can this be done? So many things crowd our lives and demand our attention. We must be about our Father's business. How can we pray constantly, always making intercession? If we remain in communion with the Son and always seek to do the things that please the Father, the concerns of our hearts are before him and he will respond to them. If you ask me to pray for you, and I rattle off an Our Father and a Hail Mary and do little else, I don't think much will be obtained. But if I take you and your concerns—and I do—into my heart and keep them there, the Lord sees them whenever I am in communion with him and most especially when I am in deepest communion with him in silent prayer, and he responds to them. This is why contemplative prayer, even though it is not thinking of particular needs but is dwelling lovingly in the deep places of God, is a most powerful intercessory prayer. In that intimate embrace, God responds to all the desires that are lodged in our hearts. We monks often marvel at the wonderful way the Lord cares for our loved ones, even though we do not often pray explicitly for them.

I think the gospels point to this. Two Marys, great women of prayer, give the example. At Cana, of which we have spoken previously, Mary made no request. She simply articulated her concern: "They have no wine" (John 2:3).

We might more easily and more confidently identify with that other Mary, if she be indeed the woman out of whom Jesus cast seven devils, she whose penitent tears washed the divine feet and whose hair dried them. After her conversion she chose the "best" part and learned the ways of silent contemplative prayer, that of sitting at the Lord's feet instead of being busy about much serving. When her hour of need arrived and a great concern pressed on her heart, she stood before the Lord and received a complete response, one beyond her expectation, but wholly in accord with it. Such prayer presupposes having sat at the Lord's feet listening to him in the gospels and, through such intimacy, being able to place complete trust in him—even to death and four days in the tomb.

Intercessory prayer is not a question of a lot of prayers; it is a question of a lot of love. He or she who loves much accomplishes much when that love is coupled with strong faith.

We had in our monastery a wonderful old laborer. Brother Pat was the last of the Irish brothers. For years he lived a rather solitary life in the potato cellars, assorting the abundant crop. But he was not alone. He prayed constantly. In his final years, Patrick's sight began to fail. In the end he was hardly able to read. But each day he would peruse the front page of the newspaper. He could make out the headlines. That was enough. He took these concerns into his heart and that was his prayer for the next twenty-four hours.

On Judgment Day it will be fascinating to see who has really accomplished what in this world of ours. The currents of prayer will stand out and we will be amazed. The greatest missionary of modern times was a very young nun who never left her Carmel in Lisieux.

Praise the Lord!

Praise him in the morning.
Praise him in the noon time.
Praise him! Praise him!
Praise him when the sun goes down.

Praise the Lord! We have seen pictures of them. We have certainly read about them. Perhaps there are some among our friends. Maybe even we have found ourselves in their midst. Praise the Lord! We call them charismatics and try to lend a certain respectability to them, now that they have come out of their tents and are in the midst, or at least on the fringe, of our own churches. The "People of Praise," they are sometimes called. They speak of being "baptized" in the Spirit—a rather ambiguous term, smacking of the heresy of rebaptism (or perhaps responding to a deep desire in our own hearts to begin the Christian life again with a new injection of warmth and enthusiasm. Praise the Lord!).

They never seem to tire of reading the Scriptures, sharing with one another, and praising God in all sorts of ways. Praise the Lord! Lunch with them will probably mean more prayer than food, more grace and thanksgiving than eating. Praise the Lord! The surge may be ebbing a bit now, but there are still enough of them who are exuberantly happy to spend an evening praising

God instead of cheering on the Boston Celtics. Praise the Lord! And...they are a challenge to us.

What are we to make of this prayer of praise? Is it important? Should praise be a part of my prayer life, my response to God?

First of all, it is important to realize that there is more than one way to praise God. Handclapping, shouting—Praise the Lord! Alleluia! Amen!—dancing, singing, "babbling" in strange sounds or unknown tongues is fine. The gift to bring our whole being into praise, to break out of our restrictive mind-sets, to forget ourselves and really celebrate God's goodness, beauty, power, and love, is *wonderful*—a real gift. But there is more than one way to confess God with our whole being. Our Quaker brother who sits in silence, attending the movement of the Spirit, resting to hear the still small voice, is giving eloquent homage to the all-ness of God. Mary was said to have chosen "the best part" when she left off doing and saying to acknowledge Christ's mastery by simply being at his feet. Some of us, like Michal, are not happy to see our Davids dance wildly before the Ark; others are scandalized to see Mary sitting there in some sort of "eastern" meditation; and some can abide by neither. We have our own longstanding tradition. Why do we need to bring in Pentecostal ways or fall into Quietism? Yes, God gave us tongues to praise him. And he also gave us reason to do it in a prudent and dignified way.

It certainly is true that the mainline Christian tradition is not lacking in its call to praise God. The official morning prayer of the Church has been called Lauds—a name derived from the Latin word *laudare,* to praise. Its confession and meditation mounts to the daily singing of those enthusiastic psalms which climax the biblical Psalter:

Praise the LORD!
Praise the LORD from the heavens;
 praise him in the heights!
Praise him, all his angels;
 praise him, all his host!

Praise him, sun and moon;
 praise him, all you shining stars!
Praise him, you highest heavens,
 and you waters above the heavens!

Let them all the name of the LORD (Psalm 148:1–4).

Praise the LORD!
Sing to the LORD a new song,
 his praise in the assembly of the faithful.
Let Israel be glad in its Maker;
 let the children of Zion rejoice in their King.
Let them praise his name
  with dancing… (Psalm 149:1–3).

Praise the LORD!
Praise God in his sanctuary;
 praise him in his mighty firmament!
Praise him for his mighty deeds;
 praise him according to his surpassing greatness!

> Praise him with trumpet sound;
>> praise him with lute and harp!
> Praise him with tambourine and dance;
>> praise him with strings and pipe!
> Praise him with clanging cymbals;
>> praise him with loud clashing cymbals!
> Let everything that breathes praise the LORD!
>> Praise the LORD! (Psalm 150:1–6).

Every day the Church sings. Do we so praise? at least in our hearts?

The morning office goes on to take up old Zechariah's Canticle: "Blessed be the Lord God of Israel," and in the evening we take up the Blessed Virgin Mary's enthusiastic hymn: "My soul proclaims the greatness of the Lord."

It is true that while more and more laypersons are joining the monks and nuns in this school of prayer and praise, the canonical offices do not directly touch the lives of most Christian people. But the eucharistic liturgy is not lacking in pouring forth its praise:

> Glory to God in the highest
>> and peace to his people on earth.
> Lord God, heavenly King,
>> almighty God and Father,
>>> we worship you, we give you thanks,
>>> we praise you for your glory.
> For you alone are the Holy One,
> you alone are the Lord,
> you alone are the Most High.

> Holy, holy, holy Lord, God of power and might,
> heaven and earth are full of your glory,
>> Hosanna in the highest.
> Blessed is he who comes in the name of the Lord,
>> Hosanna in the highest.

We do have a school of praise in our tradition. But I think we still have to admit that we are not strong in praise. This is why the enlivening challenge that has come to us from the Holy Spirit through the Pentecostal and Eastern traditions is a blessing. It calls us forth to be renewed in dimensions of our own tradition, to enter into and be receptive of the formation to be found in our own school of praise. This is not to assert that we cannot be the recipients of the good things of other traditions. The Holy Spirit, speaking to us in the Second Vatican Council, has affirmed otherwise. The Pentecostal experience and the natural forms of meditation and God-consciousness coming to us from the East can find their place within the fullness of the Christian experience. "All things are ours, and we are Christ's, and Christ is God's." Anything that helps us to acknowledge the all-ness of God and to give ourselves to him in confession of that reality is good.

Saint Bernard of Clairvaux was an outstanding master of prayer and praise. In the twelfth century he was the spiritual father of all Christendom. The pope himself was his spiritual son. All looked to him for teaching and guidance. One day the cardinal chancellor of Rome wrote to him asking for a treatise or instruction on love. Saint Bernard responded with his beautiful little work, *On the Love of God*. In the course of this practical teaching, the saint said there are four steps in the ordinary development of love. First, we are all caught up in self-love. Gradually we come to be appreciative of what God is doing for us, giving us even ourselves, so we begin to love him because of what he does for us. But as we get to know God we go beyond this. We begin to love God for his own sake, for he is good and worthy to be loved. This is praise: the acknowledgment that can be expressed in word, song, and dance. But only when it is expressed with the gift of our whole being is it what it should be. And even then, of course, it is not what is due to the infinitely good and loving God.

Praise, when we get down to it, is a matter of justice. It is truly due to God. It is the truthful and just response of our minds and hearts to what is, to who God is: the all-good, all-loving, all-merciful. It would be his due even if we were not the direct beneficiaries of all this goodness. The fact that we are makes the obligation press on us all the more, for if we are alive to what is, we experience the divine goodness most intimately. The beauty of God is imprinted in our very being, for he has made us in his own image. Through meditation, we experience this divine presence and enter into awed contemplation, our whole being confessing his all-ness. Through the gifts of the Spirit, we taste and see how good God is and our joy erupts in song and shouts or the gentle flow of heartfelt praise. The modes, the ways, vary with the times, with persons, with seasons of grace, but reality and its call remain the same. Praise him!

An openness to the immanence and transcendence of the divine goodness transforms our lives and relationships. We come to sense the activity and the effect of the divine goodness in all we perceive. We begin to appreciate each person and thing as we ought. This is a source of great joy. It calls forth more praise, love, and caring. We enjoy God's creation more and it impels us to praise him more and more.

In praise we leave off being self-centered and become God-centered. It is not that we leave our own center. But rather, no longer remaining superficially centered in our false or projected self, we plunge to the depths and find our true center, our true self, in the center of God. And we find everyone else and all else there. What occupies us now is not some puny, very vulnerable self-image that must be protected at all costs, but the magnanimous wonder of God flowing through us and all else. Our hearts beat with praise. We rejoice in all the beauty that is—no room for jealousy here. We are totally secure as the beneficiaries of divine goodness. "If God is for us, who can be against us? Is it possible that he who did not spare his own Son, but handed him over for the sake of us all, will not grant us all things besides?...I am certain that neither height nor depth, nor any other creature, will be able to separate us from the love of God that comes to us in Christ Jesus, our Lord."

When the deep conviction of the all-goodness of God takes hold of us, we find a wonderful facility to say, "Thy will be done." It becomes our deepest desire and greatest joy to be in total harmony with infinite goodness and love, even when we cannot understand the full impact or the mysterious suffering of particular dispositions. Certainly we can and do experience the fear, the grief, the pain at different levels of our being. Our Master sweat blood and was sorrowful unto death. But in the deepest there is joy at being in harmony with infinite wisdom, love, and goodness.

Scripture often puts praise and thanksgiving together. Praise seems to go beyond thanksgiving. When giving thanks, our attention is still divided. We are conscious of both the benefits we have in some way received and the benefactor. In praise it all comes together. The benefit is in the benefactor. All is his goodness. Our attention, our love, is wholly upon him.

I certainly do not want to play down thanksgiving. Thanks is due to God for all and in all. "I thank you, God, for the wonder of my being"…and your Being. Thanksgiving is often the gateway to praise. As Saint Bernard pointed out, we begin to perceive the goodness of God in his goodness to us. But then we go on to see Goodness itself and praise him.

Praise also has an intimate relation with another important dimension of prayer: reparation. It is in the light of the goodness of God, perceived and calling forth our acknowledgment, that we perceive also the heinousness of our sins and offenses, of all sin and offense. We fall to our knees, crushed by the blatant vileness of such human activity in the face of what is. We try to do anything we can to efface such blots from images that should solely reflect divine goodness and beauty. Reparation is the other face of praise. This is why they are often expressed as one in the gift of self in adoring presence. Our whole being is offered in homage, all we can do to make amends. We are yours, O God, and all that we have is yours.

The prayer of praise is important for us. But how does one develop the attitude, the ability, the inner conviction, the perception, out of which true praise flows? All prayer is a gift. We can ask for the gift of praise and open ourselves to receive it. This is what many have been moved to do through the charismatic movement, and the results have been dramatic. However, not all are drawn or graced to go that route. But all are certainly called to enter into the prayer of the Church, that great school of prayer and praise. If the average layperson does not find it possible or useful to pray the whole of the daily Office, parts of it can be used. The psalms of praise can become part of one's morning prayer. The canticles of Zachariah and Mary could conclude morning and evening reflection or meditation. The hymns of praise of the Mass can be carried over into daily life as moments of ascension.

In recent years Christian monasticism has had to face a new question or challenge. From the earliest times when a man wanted to become a monk, he went out in search of monks. He found a spiritual father or a community and began to live with him or them. He did what he saw being done, and in the doing he learned the meaning; his mind and his heart were formed. As he bowed repeatedly before the Blessed Sacrament, he came to know what it meant to worship Christ in the Eucharist. As he bowed to his abbot, he came to sense and reverence Christ's presence in him. As he washed his brothers' feet, he learned things about humility and obedience.

Recently, though, in response to a certain idea of authenticity, men have not wanted to do these things if they have not first the inner sentiments these acts are supposed to express. As you can readily see, this poses a real problem. How can we come to have these sentiments if we feel we cannot enter into the formative experience without them? It leaves us depending wholly on conceptual formation. It is true, we can by study and reflection, by openness to reality, come to the disposition of praise. This way should not be neglected. But I would put in a plea for the other path of experience, letting the external experience form the inner attitude and heart. Even if we don't feel like praising God, even if such prayers, psalms, and hymns seem unauthentic on our lips, let us enter into the prayer of the Church, and in the repetition let it form our hearts. Praise him! Praise the Lord!

Through daily repetition, a psalm like Psalm 148 will form us so that we will begin to see sun and moon, shining stars and highest heaven, with new eyes. They will call us forth to enter into their essential hymn of praise. Indeed, all creation, which in its very being hymns its loving Creator, will so call us forth, and all life will become for us a prayer of praise. Again, we will know the inner meaning of our Lord's word to pray without ceasing. Praise him! For in every breath we breathe, in all the life and energy that stirs in us, in our very being and in the being of all, he is praiseworthy and is praised. Amen. Alleluia! (which, incidentally, means: Praise Yahweh). Amen. Amen.

Who Is a
Contemplative?

A few years ago I had the privilege and responsibility of or-
ganizing and chairing an international meeting between
spiritual mothers and fathers of the Cistercian tradition and their
Orthodox counterparts. In the course of the meeting, one of the
Orthodox monks, now a bishop, related an experience he had
when as a young monk he was sent to study in London. One
Saturday afternoon, shortly after his arrival, a new friend asked
if he would like to visit a contemplative nun. The young monk
was delighted and prepared for the visit with great expectation.
He planned how he would prostrate at the feet of this holy woman,
receive her blessing and rise to kiss her hand, and then receive from
her inspired lips a word of life. He prayed the rest of the afternoon
and fasted from supper in preparation for the great event.

As the two students started out, the young monk enthusias-
tically shared his expectations with his confrere, only to be greeted
with laughter. The student then told him that the contemplative
would probably laugh even harder if she wasn't stunned into silence. When they arrived at the convent and the exuberant young
nun appeared behind the grille, a confused monk began to understand his friend's laughter.

Our Orthodox brother had immediately equivalated "contemplative" with "hesychast." For him and his tradition there is no canonical institution nominated "contemplative" or "hesychastic." The adjective belongs to a person, lay or monastic, who has attained a high degree of sanctity and union with God; one who has been privileged, usually after years of asceticism, to enter into the divine silence and experience the apophatic God.

In the West we have grown used to communities of monks and nuns who are institutionally called contemplative. The laity, devout and not so devout, and even the clergy and religious, are not wholly free from the tendency to place the members of these institutions on—if not Saint Simon's stylite—at least a bit of a pedestal. A recent TV documentary, which exposed some Trappist monks as men who had their fears, their doubts, and their hangups, disturbed and even shocked many, though for many more, the revelation was reassuring.

Who is a contemplative? A member of a canonical contemplative institute? I would say the answer should certainly be "Yes." A contemplative institute should be for contemplatives. The whole life should be structured to facilitate the daily and ultimately the constant practice of contemplation. As a vocation father I would even go so far as to say that no person should be admitted to a contemplative community who does not already practice some form of contemplative prayer daily and who does not sense a deep need to have this kind of communion with God as the central focus of his or her life.

Vocation includes, I believe, three graces: First, there is the grace to see a particular way of life as beautiful. One does not naturally regard "sitting at Jesus' feet"—a life that lays aside secular activities and apostolic ministries—as meaningful. Only by grace can one sense the value of such "waste." I have seen many parents and friends, even priests, struggle with this question. Even so, one does not naturally see the beauty of what, precisely, is sacramental marriage—a sign of Christ's love for his Church and his Church's love for him. I have often wondered how many really enter into marriage as a vocation. Perhaps this is at the heart of the widespread failure in this sublime vocation.

Then there is the second grace, the grace to see a particular vocation or vocations as beautiful for oneself. Many men who come regularly to our monastery on retreat perceive in a very deep way the beauty of the Cistercian vocation, but do not see it as a beautiful vocation for themselves. They receive the first grace, but not the second. That is usually the case with our families, if not at the outset, at least eventually. If the first grace of seeing the beauty of the different vocations in the Church is far from universal, it is still fairly widespread in the faith community. Sacramental marriage, priesthood, and monastic life are seen as beautiful vocations. Not so widespread are the second graces, yet they are common enough. Many men and women do perceive a number of vocations as beautiful for themselves. They could be good and happy spouses and parents; good and effective parish priests; good, joyful, and holy monks and nuns.

It is the third grace that is decisive: the grace to carry through effectively in embracing a particular way of life. I believe men and women must not only see the contemplative life as beautiful and as beautiful for themselves—but must also effectively practice contemplative prayer before they can consider themselves as having a call. It is important that the vocation father or mother be able to give inquirers some practical teachings so that they can begin to enter a contemplative type of prayer.

But not only those called to contemplative life are called to contemplation. That is one of the reasons why, I suspect, so many were helped and experienced a certain joy when some Cistercian Trappists revealed publicly their very human struggles. The universal call to contemplation underlined by the Second Vatican Council is being widely experienced today. In face of the common failure of parishes to provide teaching in contemplative prayer, many Catholics have turned to masters of other traditions to learn how to meditate.

Perhaps we should take a moment at this point to note a semantic concern. In our recent Catholic tradition, when we have spoken of "meditation" we have usually had in mind a discursive type of consideration and when we have spoken of "contemplation" we have had in mind a single act of presence, usually loving presence, to Reality. In Hindu terminology, as it has come over into English, these terms have the reverse sense. *Contemplation* refers to discursive consideration; *meditation* is more a means to or actual simple presence. It stands as a significant commentary on the vitality of our Christian catechesis that today in the West the Hindu terminology is the one that largely prevails among the young.

To continue with our train of thought, others, perhaps the less courageous or more faithful (each must question himself/herself), have wanted to find the fulfillment of their deep aspiration within their own Catholic tradition. But they have wondered, and perhaps have been deterred by the awe that has tended to surround the contemplative community and closed out the true humanness of the men and women within—strugglers like their sisters and brothers outside, sinners who confess regularly, but yet dare to sit at the feet of the Master and waste their life's perfume on him.

Who is a contemplative? The etymology of this word is interesting. It comes from Latin roots and Roman pagan practice. *Con*, of course, means "to be with": confrere—a brother who is with me; communion—in union with; concord—to be in accord with, to be bound up with. The pagan priests of Rome used to look to the heavens to know the will of the gods. They would perform auguries and especially watch the flight of birds through a segment of the heavens called the *templa*. In time the *templa* was projected to the earth, the *templum*—the temple, where one would go to know the will of the gods.

Contemplation is being in a state ("tion") of "being with" the *templa,* the expression of God's will, the presence of God, with God himself. "God is where his will is." The contemplative is one who lives habitually or is seeking to live habitually in union with the divine movement, the manifestation of the divine will and presence, with God himself.

All Christians have been baptized into Christ. They are called to have "the mind of Christ," their head, who sought always to do the things that pleased the Father. Christ, our head and master, was indeed a contemplative. And all his members and disciples are called to follow him in this.

Who is a contemplative? The answer is: Every true Christian; everyone who is truly living in harmony with his nature as a person baptized into Christ. If we truly want union with God we are not content to be united with him in doing what he wants, nor in talking to him in prayer and praise; we want to be truly one with him in himself, to experience a oneness with him. And we need this to energize and ground our oneness with him in action and speech. This is where the particular type of prayer we call "contemplation" or "contemplative prayer" comes in. We need times when we stop doing or talking, to simply be with—to sit at the feet of Jesus or rest in his loving embrace.

The contemplative is one who practices contemplative prayer. If our prayer is authentic contemplative prayer, a being with the Source of all life and love, it necessarily overflows into our life in that we always seek the things that please the Father. We may, indeed, be weighed down by our weaknesses, our doubts, our fears, and we may often fail, but we do seek. When we sit at the feet of the Lord he may seem more absent than present, but we do sit, wasting our time on him, longing to experience his presence, his love, his very self.

Those who accept the vocation to enter a contemplative community are those who have decided to respond to an invitation, a call, to make this sitting the primary and principal activity of their lives. They are called to do this and to do it for the whole Church, organically and prophetically. The Church is a body; we are all members. Each member has his or her role. This is the role of the member who embraces the vocation to live within a contemplative community: to be a member who sits at the master's feet and energizes the whole body's will to be contemplative by the inner workings of organic grace and the outer power of prophetic witness.

It is an awesome thing to take on the responsibility of the contemplative role in the body of Christ. One who does accept it should in time, by God's grace-produced fidelity, come to be worthy, not only of the awe that is generally accorded the members of contemplative institutes, but of that special awe that excited the heart of the young Orthodox monk.

But the awe should not be a distancing awe. It should be an awe made the greater because it is clearly seen that the one who is so faithful to the contemplative dimension of life is one who is burdened by all the weaknesses of Adam's children. The great contemplatives were very human and very close. One thinks immediately of the rich humanity of a singing, dancing, asking, and complaining Teresa of Ávila; of a Bernard of Clairvaux who could write letters that still burn the pages, bewail unrequited love, and list enough physical maladies to distress any doctor. It is these true contemplatives, so fully human, who give the rest of us hope that by being faithful to spending our time in sitting at the feet of Jesus, resting in the presence, we will come to experience not only transient moments of contemplative union, but a life of contemplation, a state of being with the *templa,* the manifesting presence of God, with God himself.

The Contemplative Attitude

In some ways our globe is ever growing smaller. We are placed in almost immediate contact with every hopeful and anguished pulsation of its teeming life. But in some ways our world grows ever larger. Our scientists reach out beyond the known galaxies and probe the depths of the mysterious black holes. Of one thing we are sure, in many ways our lives move ever faster as day by day, hour by hour, extremely sophisticated technology accelerates our knowledge, our needs, our mobility, and our consumption. In the face of this increasing—and increasingly—frenetic activity, something deep within us, like a drowning man struggling in the midst of a turbulent and engulfing sea, desperately seeks for a stable refuge where we can find ourselves centered in quiet presence. Hence the significantly increased interest in meditation in our own country and in general in the developed countries in the West. In the face of great and constant turbulence, we can escape total dissipation of our life's energies and the loss of our true selves only if there are moments and spaces when we can come home to ourselves.

This is an important consideration. Still it is not an adequate consideration. The human mind, a wonderful image of the divine, has an infinite capacity and thirst for the true; the human heart can be satisfied with nothing less than all good. A restlessness, a frustration, will plague us until we find the way and know that the path to infinite truth and goodness lies open to us.

Again, though, this is not enough for persons whose being has been graced, whose minds have been strengthened and expanded for and by intimate divine knowing, and whose hearts are called to divine intimacy: "I do not call you servants any longer...but I have called you friends" (John 15:15). For us, the lively potential and aspiration of our being, of who we are and what we aspire to and need, suffer frustration inevitably experienced, even if not clearly perceived, if our presence to the creation, its life and its activity, is not made integral by a communication, involving a personal and loving interaction, with the divine creating presence.

To be fully alive, to operate according to our full potential, to be unfrustrated in our aspirations, to be challenged to ever more expansive life, we Christians need to be constantly touching reality in all its fullness. To express this in another way, we need to be operating at the level of those gifts of the Holy Spirit received at baptism or at the moment when we came into the gracious state of participation in personalized divine life.

When God creates he does not, like the human creative person, employ previously created material. Because the material we employ in our creative activity participates in being, our "creativity" simply modifies it. The material is able to stand in being independently of us; so when we complete our "creative" modifications, we can leave the product and it will continue to be, without our sustaining presence. A carpenter takes some fine oak wood, makes a handsome table, sets it on its own legs and walks away. He may never see it again, or even think of it. It may pass through many hands or be totally neglected. Yet it will continue to stand.

When God creates he employs no previously created material. He calls something or someone into being by sharing with it or him something of his own being, goodness, and beauty. This is why everything and everyone who is, is both good and beautiful. Because God's creative act is essentially participative, it can never cease, or the created ceases. Thus every thing and every person that is, is right now because God is at this very moment bringing it or him or her into being, sharing with his creature something of his own being, goodness, and beauty. Ultimately, apart from God there is nothing that is. All that is, is, because it participates in some varying degree in God's being.

When Saint Benedict's biographer, Pope Saint Gregory the Great, wished to summarize Benedict's spiritual outlook, he recounted an incident in the life of the great monk. One evening Saint Benedict retired to his cell to pray. As he prayed by the window he suddenly had a vision. He perceived the whole of creation as it were under a single ray of divine light. What Gregory wished to teach is that Benedict, through contemplation, achieved a united perception of reality.

If we adequately perceive any thing or any person, we perceive not only the person or thing but also our God of creative love bringing the person or the thing forth in his love and also the person's or thing's oneness with ourselves in this. As persons in charity, enlivened by a loving orientation to God, our adequate response to each created person and thing must involve a loving communication with the divine actuality present at the ground of their being.

The whole of creation is made unto the glory of its maker, our God, to be a praise of his glory. The rest of creation has been given over to us so that it might give expression to its praise through our minds and hearts. We are the high priests of creation—a role we adequately fulfill only when we perceive the divinely created goodness and beauty of each creature and reverently refer it back to its maker. Perception of the whole of creation, ourselves included, as constantly coming forth from the divine creative love and returning thereto in glorifying praise, through the fulfillment of being what we are supposed to be, gives a coherent unifying direction to all that enters into our lives.

The reality then of what we are as human, graced persons situated in the created order postulates a depth of perception and relation which can be neglected only at the price of superficiality, frustration, and a dispersion of our vitality and sense of directedness. To achieve this quality of perception and relation, we have to be truly with what we are about, hear in its fullness the reality present to us, at each moment, and not be ahead of ourselves or behind ourselves, missing the present reality because we are planning or anticipating what lies ahead or are unable to let go of the past.

My spiritual father used to quote to me the dictum: "The past and the future are only other forms of self. God is *now*." This is not to deny that there are times when we should be planning for the future and envisioning and determining goals, but when this is the case, the planning and projecting become the "now," because they are what we are now supposed to be doing and to be present to. The future takes us from the present and reality—and God—when it takes us from attentiveness to what we are presently doing, where we presently are. And so also, the past.

Not only the past and the future, but any involvement in the thoughts and images that are flowing through our minds and imaginations, which are extraneous to our present concern, draw us away, prevent us from being truly present, induce superficiality, and keep us from responding to the fullness of the creative divine presence. If we engage in interior dialog with these byproducts of self, we cannot give more than divided attention to the divine speaking to us immediately in the inner silence or through the person or thing that is calling for attention at the moment. This is not to deny that there are times when we can and should attend to our thoughts and images. At such times they become the due objects of our attention in which and through which the divine is present and speaking. What we are pointing to here is the division, voluntary or involuntary, of our attention, which prevents depth and wholeness in our response. When we touch the ground of being in anyone or anything, including ourselves, we touch God, and in God, all else. This is the source of universal compassion.

We may then perceive our continual desire and aspiration to be in touch with the fullness of reality and responsive to the divine Presence at all times, and we may consciously espouse it. In other words we may want to have a contemplative attitude toward life. Then comes the practical question: How do we achieve this?

Active or discursive meditation seems to be able to take us only so far. We may ponder reality and formulate determination to respond wholistically to each person and each thing we are to encounter in the course of the day. But our examen in the evening will constantly reveal a paucity of success. We will perhaps at freer, more lively, or more challenging moments achieve a certain integrity in our response, but for the most part our day will find our minds taken up with the phenomena of the moment, both the central and the peripherial, and relatively little mindfulness of the divine creative force sustaining those phenomena, and their relatedness in depth to our own being and the being of all else. Perhaps the greatest and most effective fruit coming out of discursive meditation on this reality will be a deeper desire to live in a contemplative mode, to live from the center, and fervent prayer to God to bring about the fulfillment of this desire.

Far more effective, both as more integral existential prayer and as dispositive acts, are periods of contemplative presence and prayer. It matters little whether we go about this consciously employing a method, such as centering prayer, or in some natural way of our own—which will usually involve some sort of method. The important thing is that we begin to open up space in our lives to be wholly present and receptive to the divine creative and loving presence. I do not mean to imply that moments—even long ones—of contemplative presence cannot spontaneously overtake us, naturally and supernaturally. We have all, I hope, had such experiences. But if we simply wait for such moments to occur on their own, they will be few and far between, and our progress will be slow indeed.

On the other hand, while God does touch us at times without any previous acts on our part, as it were to entice us, ordinarily, respecting as he does the freedom he gives, he does not invade our lives without our asking or seeking: "Ask, and it will be given you; search, and you will find" (Matthew 7:7).

In this regard God does not listen to our lips, but to our hearts. We ask more by our actions than by our words. We seek more by making space for response. By taking time regularly to let go of our usual attention to our thoughts and images, and being simply present, we begin to be in touch with that level of reality where we and all else are at every moment coming forth in the creative love of God. We touch the ground of being, the center. Coming to our own center, we pass through it into the center of God, the center of all.

Because this is an experience beyond thought and image, at first it is difficult for us to sense that it is really happening. As Saint Teresa expressed it:

> ...the soul is doubtful as to what has really happened until it has had a good deal of experience of it. It wonders if the whole thing was imagination, if it has been asleep...it retains a thousand misgivings....
>
> *INTERIOR CASTLE*, FIFTH MANSION

But if we persevere in this practical seeking, making time and space, we will begin to perceive the fruit in our lives. And this is the way our master told us to evaluate things—we are to judge a tree by its fruit.

Getting in touch regularly with infinite love and experiencing how that love brings us forth, and all else with us, at every moment, we cannot but love him the more, love ourselves the more, so affirmed by the divine, and love everyone else the more. What joy floods our lives in this experience of love! There is peace, for all is coming into order. And patience, for God is creatively at work in us, in others, in the whole creative project. How can we but be kind to others, realizing this and their intimate oneness with us? Goodness marks our every response. We trust God and others. We are gentle and caring. We treat all that is created, our own bodies, and all that is given for our use, with due reverence and concern. (This attitude, I might add, seems to me to be the only possible basis for a true ecology.) These are the fruits of the Spirit: "love, joy, peace, patience, kindness, generosity, faithfulness, gentleness, and self-control" (Galatians 5:22–23).

We do not meditate only to enjoy a few minutes of transcendent peace. For us, as Christians, if meditation is to be what it should be—prayer—we are not mainly seeking something for ourselves. We are seeking God. But such seeking of God, such experience of him, brings about in us by his activity a transformation of consciousness with a prevailing contemplative attitude. When in the time of meditation we experience the ground of being, that center where God in his creative love is bringing us all forth, we begin to acquire as it were a connatural sensitivity to this reality. It begins to pervade the whole of our lives and all our relations. We begin to sense the ever-present divine causality, the divine presence that lies under the phenomena. We read within, as it were, and even begin to taste, to savor, the present divine goodness. This is the operation of what Catholic theology has traditionally called the gifts of the Holy Spirit. This level of consciousness and activity does not come about through our conscious efforts, but as an overflow from our contemplative experience of God through the working of the Holy Spirit within our spirit. This is essentially the contemplative attitude.

A contemplative attitude does not come about in our lives simply by the daily practice of some method of meditation, such as centering prayer, or sitting each day gazing at flowers or sunsets. We are all too capable of perverting such practices into narcissistic self-seeking gratification. We can seek peace for our own sake and achieve a false peace that has more to do with apathy and unreality than entering into the divine order of caring love. A true contemplative attitude, and a practice which nurtures it, is grounded in an integral life; for a Christian, an integral Christian life. Our master has said: "If any want to become my followers, let them deny themselves and take up their cross daily and follow me" (Luke 9:23).

We must hear the Lord, our master. This implies daily listening to the gospels, fidelity to spiritual reading. Faith comes through hearing. An active and lively faith enables us to perceive our true nature and aspirations, and motivates us to that activity, the development of a contemplative attitude, which will fulfill our aspirations. A certain asceticism is a prerequisite here. The asceticism of making time for reading and meditation. But more important, the asceticism within the meditation and the contemplative attitude. We cannot let things go, we cannot let ourselves go, our more superficial selves with our thoughts, feelings, and images, in order to attend to the deeper reality, to the divine presence, if these things have a real hold on us. We have to be able in some way to let go of the pursuit of the things of this world, the possession of them, and die to ourselves, in order to be able to live unto God. We have to be able to waste time on God. Following this way, we come to realize, like Saint Paul, we are "poor, yet making many rich; as having nothing, and yet possessing everything" (2 Corinthians 6:10). "All belong to you, and you belong to Christ, and Christ belongs to God" (1 Corinthians 3:22–23).

Giving time to our contemplative prayer, developing a contemplative attitude, will never detract from our apostolic efficacy; it will only enhance it. We will bring to every person and every situation, a new energy, caring, and love, a new openness and compassion, a new power in the Holy Spirit to enlighten, affirm, and heal. Knowing wherein our true happiness lies, we will be able effectively to show others the way. Having possession of the inner way, we will be able to open to the poor, who desperately need to hear it, the mysterious Good News that blessed are they, for theirs is the kingdom of heaven. We are all poor.

Let us come at this from another angle for a moment. We all seek happiness. We are made for happiness. The *Catechism of the Catholic Church* assures us of this. It is the message of the whole of the Good News—almost too good to be true. Such gratuitous love is beyond our ordinary experience. We find it hard to believe, and often deny it by the way we act, proclaiming by our actions that we know better than the Creator what is to our happiness, that his directives are not really to our happiness.

We are made for happiness. Each of us, like Charlie Brown, has our own definition of happiness. Let me share mine with you again. Happiness consists in knowing what we want, and knowing that we have it or are on the way to getting it. We do have a certain freedom in choosing what we want out of life. Many people are unhappy because they are unwilling to choose. Every choice implies giving up something. When a man marries, he chooses one woman, and gives up all other women. The decision not to choose (made explicitly or implicitly) involves giving up commitment. Commitment in love is the only way to full human happiness. We are free to choose, but we must choose within certain perimeters, respecting reality. If we choose the impossible, we doom ourselves to frustration. A mute cannot put his happiness in being an opera singer. Only a lunatic chooses the moon. But our choice must also respect and fulfill the exigencies of our nature—our human nature, our Christ-person, our particular gifts and talents and needs. To ignore this really means frustration.

It is here that a contemplative attitude is imperative. For it is only a contemplative attitude that is habitually perceptive of one's true potential and aspirations and guides a life in response to them. The contemplative person knows what he truly wants, knows that in large measure he already has it, and knows that he is en route to possessing it fully. Contemplative monasteries house some of the happiest people in the world. And this world is graced with some contemplative persons who convey the whole meaning of monasteries in the way they center all things in God and live out of that radiant loving center.

Jesus, Our Teacher
of Prayer

The disciples of our Lord one day approached him. They had been observing John the Baptizer. There was a certain jealousy among the disciples of the two great teachers. Their hearts needed to be purified and the roles of their masters clarified. Those who had opted to follow Jesus were sure he was the one, or at least wanted to be sure. They wanted Jesus to be all that John was and more. Among other things, John was teaching his disciples to pray, and so Jesus' disciples wanted their teacher to teach them to pray too.

Jesus could be said to have been a prayerful man—a man whose life was marked with prayer. As a devout Jew this was to be expected. Morning and evening prayer, prayer at meals, services in the synagogue, the Sabbath observance, the pilgrimages—these are all part of the rich heritage we have received from our Jewish forebears and which were a part of the everyday life of Joseph and Mary and their son, Jesus. But when Jesus reached the appropriate age and struck out on his own as a teaching rabbi, prayer marked his life even more strongly. Jesus always taught by example as well as by word.

Jesus began his teaching mission with forty days in solitude.

The gospels emphasize the temptations and combat with the evil one, but we may be sure that he who "was led up by the Spirit into the wilderness" (Matthew 4:1)—and reminded his adversary that you must "worship the Lord your God, and serve only him" (Matthew 4:10)—spent this time in worship and communion with the Father. The gospels are more explicit about his prayer before the more decisive moments of his mission. "He spent the night in prayer to God" (Luke 6:12) before he selected his chosen twelve from among his disciples. He led three of them—Peter, James, and John—up a high mountain to pray before he manifested to them his transfiguring glory and illumined them with the Taboric light. It was these same three he invited, rather unsuccessfully, to share his deepest experience in prayer in Gethsemane before he embarked upon the consummation of his mission.

As the evangelist Luke has especially brought out, prayer marked all the most significant moments of his life. It was "when Jesus also had been baptized and was praying the heaven was opened, and the Holy Spirit descended upon him in bodily form like a dove. And a voice came from heaven, 'You are my Son, the Beloved; with you I am well pleased'" (Luke 3:21–22). It was when he "was praying alone, with only the disciples near him," that he put the question to them, "Who do you say that I am?" and evoked Peter's great confession: "The Messiah of God" (Luke 9:20). It was the Father who taught this to Peter in response to Jesus' prayer.

Jesus knew the Father to be the source of all the power and goodness that flowed through him and surrounded his ministry, and he praised and thanked him. "Filled with joy by the Holy Spirit, he said, 'I bless you, Father, Lord of heaven and earth, for hiding these things from the learned and the clever and revealing them to mere children (unless you become as children, you cannot enter in). Yes, Father, for that is what it pleased you to do.'" In praying thus, Jesus was clearly conscious of his teaching mission, of giving us an example. Before his greatest miracle, prior to and prefiguring his own resurrection, the raising up of Lazarus (four days dead), Jesus prayed: "Father, I thank you for having heard me. I knew that you always hear me, but I have said this for the sake of the crowd standing here..." (John 11:41–42).

Saint Benedict, that great disciple of Jesus and master of millions, tells his disciples: "And first of all, whatever good work you undertake, pray most urgently that the Lord will bring it to completion." If the very Son of God prayed to the Father in the accomplishment of his works, how much more ought we, sons and daughters of God, initiate our works with heartfelt, confident, imploring prayer!

And when his works were done and his energies spent, Jesus felt the need to go apart for refreshing prayer. After his first great day of miracles in Capernaum, he "went up to a lonely place and prayed there." And when he fed five thousand men, plus women and children, with four loaves and two fish, he sent the crowds away and "went up into the hills by himself to pray." When his apostles returned, enthusiastic but weary, from their first mission, he sought to take them apart "where they could be by themselves."

Jesus' prayer was marked by simplicity and directness. Again and again he raised his eyes to heaven and cried, "Father," whether in the joy of raising his friend or in the anguish of his own bitter agony. He was aware of the power of such prayer and fully confident: "Do you think I cannot ask my Father and he will promptly send more than twelve legions of angels to defend me." Something in him did want to pray for his own deliverance, for things to be the way which humanly seemed best. "What shall I say? Father, save me from this hour?" But such prayer was always conditional. "Father, if you are willing, take this cup away from me." In the end his prayer was, "Father, glorify your name." "Let your will be done, not mine." And with greatest confidence he concluded his life, "Father, into your hands I commend my spirit."

Jesus was conscious of the importance of praying for others, of his mediatorial role. He prayed for his apostles and especially for Peter. "I have prayed for you, Simon." But he prayed "not only for these, but for those also who through their words will believe," all Christian peoples. And he prayed, too, for those who would not believe. "Father, forgive them, for they know not what they do." He prayed that we might receive the Holy Spirit, who would make his teaching efficacious in us: "I shall ask the Father, and he will give you another advocate to be with you forever, the Spirit of truth…the Advocate, the Holy Spirit, whom the Father will send in my name, will teach you everything and remind you of all I have said to you."

It was when they were moved by Jesus' example that his disciples asked for explicit teaching on prayer: "He was praying in a certain place, and after he had finished, one of his disciples said to him, 'Lord, teach us to pray, as John taught his disciples'" (Luke 11:1). And Jesus responded with that formula which we have come to call the Lord's Prayer, or the Our Father. It is much more than a formula; it is a whole school of prayer.

In the centering prayer method we suggest that at the end of the twenty minutes of contemplative prayer, the meditator pray interiorly the Lord's Prayer, slowly letting each phrase unfold. Anyone who has done this over a period of time quickly begins to realize how this formula is truly a whole school of prayer. Every kind of prayer is taught in it, and all the attitudes of prayer. There is prayer of intimacy, of praise, of submission, of petition, of reparation and contrition. We learn our own true being, as sons and daughters of the Father, one with the only Son and in solidarity with all the other children of the Father. We touch upon all our basic needs, but in the context of the wisdom of conditional prayer, for "your Father knows what you need before you ask him" (Matthew 6:8). We are constantly stretched out beyond our own immediate needs to the needs of all, of all the kingdom, now and in the eschaton, The mind, the attitude of the Son is formed in us in accord with our true baptismal nature. Easily, a whole book can be written on this teaching prayer, and it has been done often enough.

One day an elderly nun asked Saint Teresa of Ávila how she might become a contemplative. That great contemplative and teacher of prayer replied, "Sister, say the 'Our Father,' but take an hour to say it." In response to Jesus' prayer we have received the Advocate to teach us. Sitting in the school of the Lord's Prayer, we will indeed learn everything there is to learn about prayer.

Far more than content, our Lord was concerned about attitude in prayer. Indeed, the whole warp of life is the content of our prayer, for we are commanded to "stay awake, praying at all times for the strength to survive all that is going to happen and to stand with confidence before the Son of Man." It is the woof, the attitude, that makes all prayer, and makes our times of explicit prayer, true, efficacious and pleasing to God.

For our divine teacher, the attitude that is most displeasing and most undermines true prayer is hypocrisy. For this reason, while he decries those who "love to stand and pray in the synagogues and at the street corners, so that they will be seen by others" (Matthew 6:5), he counsels, "whenever you pray, go into your room and shut the door and pray to your Father who is in secret" (Matthew 6:6). This teaching should not be pushed to an extreme. Our Lord himself gave the example of praying also in public. We should not pray in public *to be seen*, but we should not be ashamed to pray in public. We should take an active, open part in public worship. Prayer before and after meals should not be relegated to the privacy of our home. It has its place at every meal. Our Lord "raised his eyes to heaven and said the blessing" in the midst of thousands. If those with whom we are breaking bread are not believers whom we can ask to join us in prayer, we can at least quietly pause for interior prayer before and after, perhaps inviting all to moments of silent presence. It is appreciated. We must not be afraid of giving public witness to our life of prayer. At the same time we must not restrict our prayer to times of public or formal prayer. We will not be able to pray with any real depth or sincerity at such times if we have not prayed to our Father in secret. In the secret communings of our heart, we truly hear the Lord, learn from the Spirit, learn how to pray.

There is another admonition of the Lord which needs to be understood properly: "When you are praying, do not heap up empty phrases as the Gentiles do; for they think that they will be heard because of their many words" (Matthew 6:7). Our Lord is certainly not inveighing here against the use of repetitious prayer, such as the rosary, ejaculations, or even the use of a prayer word or mantra. The charge is against vain repetition, meaningless rattling on, quantity instead of quality. Indeed, in that poignant little parable about the persistent widow, where our Lord does not hesitate to depict himself as a hardhearted judge, and in that other story of the importunate friend who comes in the night, our Lord praises persistent repetitive asking: "persistence will be enough to make him get up...ask...seek...knock...."

I cannot begin in a short chapter to give anything like an adequate summary of the deep, beautiful, varied and most rich teaching of our teacher of prayer. At this point I would like to urge you to turn to the teacher himself. First, you might go to those favorite passages you know so well and listen to them again: Matthew 6 or Luke 11, or whatever they are for you. But then you might turn to a biblical concordance, and look at the texts listed under pray, praying, and prayer in Matthew, Mark, Luke, and John. Then perhaps turn to "Father" in the gospels and listen to Jesus praying most intimately. Learn from the master himself, by word and example. You might find a certain excitement creeping in, a renewed attitude toward prayer as you are touched by this teacher and his advocate who dwells within.

Our whole life is to be prayer as was the life of Jesus. There is the prayer of service. There is also the prayer of petition. There is the prayer of contemplative presence, of listening, of being with.

The prayer of service is important. "I seek always to do the things that please the Father." "The Father works until now and I work." The prayer of petition is more important. "The harvest is plentiful, but the laborers are few; therefore ask the Lord of the harvest to send out laborers into his harvest" (Matthew 9:37–38). The Lord did not tell the disciples to roll up their sleeves and get to work, but first to pray for laborers, which might well have included them (and *de facto* did). First, prayer, then service. The prayer of contemplative presence is most important. "Mary has chosen the better part" (Luke 10:42). Prayer must not be monological—we doing all the talking. It must be dialogical. We need to learn to listen to God—and the more we listen, the better, for what he has to say is far more significant than anything we have to say. How can we sincerely pray, "Thy will be done," if we make no effort to hear what it is? How can we pray as we ought if we have not been taught?

We have, in the Lord Jesus, a magnificent teacher of prayer. Let us each day sit at his feet and say with the disciple, "Lord, teach us how to pray."

Mary, Teach Us
How to Pray

There is no one who knows us as well as God—after all, he is making us! He knows us inside and out, upside and down; he knows all our hopes and aspirations, our deepest needs. And he has in his own most beautiful way responded to all of them. Not the least of these thoughtful caring gifts is the almost unbelievable gift of a mother—his own mother. Mary is our mother as truly as any mother can ever be a mother. She bore us in Christ, our head—with whom we are so profoundly one. She bore us in the indescribable pains of Calvary. And she cares for us in obedience to a most loving command, the only command her divine son gave her, his most precious death-wish: "Mother, behold your son."

It is connatural for a child to learn to pray at his or her mother's knee. Indeed, if prayer is not learned there—that is where Jesus learned it—it will be an altogether different struggle to learn how to pray. We turn to Mary to acquire a deeper understanding of what we intuitively learned there. If we have not been so blessed as to have knelt at such a school of prayer, we can turn to Mother Mary to fill up that lacuna in the most consonant way possible.

Mary teaches us how to pray just as any mother does—by example. In the gospel scene where we first encounter Mary she gives us the first and most important lesson, the first objective of all prayer: to know God's will in order to say a complete "Yes" to it.

A frightened maiden is suddenly confronted by a heavenly being and a message of sublimity. Gabriel, one of God's mightiest spirits, stands before her and speaks things unheard of:

> "You will conceive in your womb and bear a son, and you will name him Jesus. He will be great, and will be called the Son of the Most High, and the Lord God will give to him the throne of his ancestor David. He will reign over the house of Jacob forever, and of his kingdom there will be no end" (Luke 1:31–33).

Mary's response was a faith-full one. There was no hesitation to believe. She wanted to do what was asked of her. All she sought was to know the way so she could respond as God wanted: "How can this be?" (Luke 1:34).

First of all in prayer we seek to know what God wants of us, to understand his love and its call, the call that has brought us into being in creation, that has made us his most dear and most beautiful children in re-creation—the call to life and love and transcendent greatness. Hearing that call, our prayer then is, "How?" In each day's journey along the path, "How?" How are we to walk to be worthy of who we are and of that to which we are called? Our journey, no less than Mary's, is absolutely unique. We are the products of a unique love, called to a unique greatness and beauty. Only the divine designer, the creative Spirit, knows the fullness of that to which we are called and the way thereto:

> "What no eye has seen, nor ear heard,
>   nor the human heart conceived,
> what God has prepared for those who love him"—
> these things God has revealed to us through the Spirit;
> for the Spirit searches everything, even the depths of
> God (1 Corinthians 2:9–10).

The angel responded to Mary's inquiry. God will always answer us. "Ask, and it will be given you; search, and you will find" (Matthew 7:7). "The Holy Spirit will come upon you, and the power of the Most High will overshadow you" (Luke 1:35).

Ultimately this is always God's answer. He will accomplish in us all that he wants of us. We have only to assent. God made us. But he not only made us, he reverences us. He knows the greatest thing he gives us is our freedom. For herein lies our power to love, the one thing he wants of us. So he completely respects our freedom. He will never force his way into our lives. "Behold, I stand at the door and knock. *If* a person opens, I will come in…." In prayer God gives us the grace to will and to do what he reveals to us is to be done. By his grace and with his gift of freedom we are able to say with the All-Holy One: "I, the servant of the Lord; let it be done with me according to your word" (Luke 1:38).

And God comes to us in a new and fuller way.

Prayer not only brings about our own transformation through the empowerment it gives us to know and be completely one with the holy will of God. It also sends us to transform the

lives of others. "Mary set out and went with haste…" (Luke 1:38).
As we see the grace of God working powerfully in our own lives
and through us in the lives of others—"as soon as I heard the
sound of your greeting, the child in my womb leaped for joy,"
Elizabeth prophesied—we need to learn from Mary another form
of prayer, that fuller and more selfless mode of thanksgiving that
is praise:

> "My soul magnifies the Lord,
>> and my spirit rejoices in God my Savior,
> for he has looked with favor on the lowliness
>>> of his servant.
>> Surely, from now on all generations
>>> will call me blessed;
> for the Mighty One has done great things for me,
>> and holy is his name.
> His mercy is for those who fear him
>> from generation to generation…" (Luke 1:46–50).

True humility does not consist in denying or hiding our true
greatness. We are great. We are fantastic! We are made in the very
image of God himself. We are the pinnacle of creation. And even
beyond that. By baptism we are made God's own children—one
with the very Son of God, in a oneness we shall never fully com-
prehend, a oneness like unto the oneness of Father, Son, and Holy
Spirit—partakers in the divine nature. We are the deified children of God. Humility does not hide this. It proudly—and yet so
humbly (for the difference between what we are and the way we
habitually act gives us much cause for humility)—proclaims its
true greatness *and* the source of that greatness. We have been

generally quite weak in our prayer of praise. It is something we do need to learn. The Holy Spirit has been teaching it to the Church in a powerful way in our time through what we have come to call the Charismatic Movement. Here men and women have learned to spend time joyfully in proclaiming God's goodness and all his other attributes and his very self. The liturgy, the Church's ever-present school of prayer, has constantly taught this. The psalms of praise, which Jesus and Mary used, are repeated again and again. Each day the evening prayer comes to completion by inviting us to sing with Mary and the whole Church her beautiful hymn of praise. Once again we are beginning to dance with Miriam on the farther shores of the Red Sea, with King David before the holy Ark.

Each of us might begin to compose our own hymns and canticles of praise, do our own dances before the Lord, praising him with body as well as word, thought, and mind. In the end we will praise him with being, lapsing into the silence of totally satisfied presence, sitting at his feet as did another Mary and then standing at his cross with the three Marys—a homage of praise when all had abandoned him, a homage that others could see only as unmitigated grief, the homage of a *fiat*, a "yes," that went beyond words unto total being.

But what about the prayer of petition—the prayer that most spontaneously comes to our lips—that tends to dominate the prayer life of most of us? Mary teaches us here too, and teaches us the right way to do it. So often, in our prayer of petition, we act as if we are convinced that we know better than God; that he needs to be told the right way for things to be done. It is *our* will that is to be done on earth and in heaven.

We also suffer from another deception, at least some of us,

some of the time. It is the idea that we do not need to bother God about the details of life. We can handle them ourselves. They are not big enough for his notice. Especially the details that are, so to speak, extras—the little things that minister to our pleasure: a beautiful sunset at the end of that special day; that the icing on the birthday cake will flow just right; that the roses, enough of them, will be budding for May Day....

Mary our Mother shows us not only how to go about our prayer of petition, but also that it can be for the little extras that make the day perfect—even some more booze for the boys when they have drunk the house dry.

> There was a wedding in Cana of Galilee, and the mother of Jesus [our Mother] was there. Jesus and his disciples had also been invited to the wedding. When the wine gave out, the mother of Jesus said to him, "They have no wine." And Jesus said to her, "Woman, what concern is that to you and me? My hour has not yet come." His mother said to the servants [and to us], "Do whatever he tells you" (John 2:1–5).

In bringing her need, Mary identifies with the needs of others and makes them her own. When others ask us to pray for them and their needs, it will accomplish little if we just rattle off a few prayers for them. God does not listen to the words of our mouth. He looks to our heart. We must bring the needs of others into our heart and make them truly our own if we really want to pray for them. In bringing her need, Mary does not tell our Lord what to do about it. She simply places it before him with total confidence in his goodness, wisdom, and power.

Later, another Mary will follow her example: "[Lazarus] whom you love is ill" (John 11:3). Naturally she might have expected a cure. She got so much more; Christ's greatest miracle before and prefiguring his own resurrection, the resurrection of a man three days dead. And here Mary gets the best of wine in abundance. Her Son's initial unresponsiveness, if not negativity, does not put her off. She proceeds with complete confidence. Mary teaches us to place our needs simply before God with complete confidence in his goodness and wisdom, confident that he in his own good time will take care of the matter in the way he knows is best for all concerned. "We know that all things work together for good for those who love God."

We don't need to tell God how to handle the matter. We don't want to insist that it be done our way—and right now. "Not my will, but thine be done" is a part of every good prayer. "Do whatever *he tells you.*" Mary confidently left the whole matter in Jesus' hands. It is her need. He loves her infinitely. He will take care of it.

So also for us and our needs. Our prayer of petition needs to be more a taking of needs deeply into our heart and being before God with them rather than a lot of words and insistence. Mary did not repeat her petition over and over again—even in the face of apparent indifference or refusal. In fact, she did not even formulate a petition; she simply expressed a need: "They have no wine," and confidently left the rest to Jesus. This is the way our mother teaches us to pray.

This basic teaching of Mary is enough for a whole life of prayer. We really need no more. In the Acts of the Apostles we see Mary continuing her instruction by example:

All these were constantly devoting themselves to prayer, together with certain women, including Mary the mother of Jesus… (Acts 1:14).

But later on, in the course of the centuries, as Mary returned again and again to visit her children, she spoke much of prayer. Many volumes can be and have been written on this powerful teaching. Most significantly, Mary has placed in our hands a string of beads, the wonderful gift of the rosary. Every religious tradition has had its beads. It seems to powerfully integrate a person's prayer when he can finger beads in union with the words of his lips and the prayer of his heart, whether it be the soft black wool beads woven with symbolic knots that our Orthodox brothers and sisters use with the Jesus Prayer, or the curious string of glass beads with its pendants that the Tibetan Lama uses to count his two hundred thousand mantras.

Mary's beads are very special. They are meant to lead to a deep prayerful experience of the central realities of Christian being. They take us again and again to the holy places and the holy events. The beads themselves seem to forge a tight bond with Mary in her own powerful prayer and experience of these mysteries, from which flow forth life and hope. I know a holy abbot, a man of transcendent contemplative prayer. But in the most anguished moments of his life I have always found him with the beads in his hands. I have never seen a brother monk close his eyes in death without the beads in his hands. When I published my first book on contemplative prayer I sent a copy to an aunt, a highly successful and gifted woman. She complimented me on the book, and concluded: "But I'll stick with the rosary."

I know a wonderful woman of love. She left high school early, for all she wanted to do was give herself in love as wife, mother, grandmother, friend, and confidante. When the years finally caught up with her and a failing health allowed for little activity, she would sit at her window, which happened to look out upon a hospital. And then, through the day she would "tell her beads" for all those she loved—really the whole world—and especially those in the hospital rooms across the way. She wondered at times why it took her so long to make the round of the beads, sometimes hours. If I had told her she was enjoying a more contemplative prayer she would probably have responded, "Nonsense, I only say my beads. I'm no contemplative." But in Mary's school of prayer, this mother learned all there is to learn about prayer. She learned to hold all the world before the Lord in compassionate love. The rosary is a great school of prayer.

In this book I have shared a lot of words about prayer. And you have patiently absorbed them. Thank you. But if you really want to learn how to pray, how to meet the challenge of prayer, turn to our Mother Mary and humbly and simply say, "Mary, teach me how to pray."

Appendixes

THE METHOD OF *LECTIO*

It is well to keep the sacred Scriptures enthroned in our home in a place of honor as a real presence of the word in our midst.

1. Take the sacred text with reverence and call upon the Holy Spirit.
2. For ten minutes (or longer, if you are so drawn) listen to the Lord speaking to you through the text, and respond to him.
3. At the end of the time, choose a word or phrase (perhaps one will have been "given" to you) to take with you, and thank the Lord for being with you and speaking to you.

More briefly we might put it this way:

1. Come into the presence and call upon the Holy Spirit.
2. Listen for ten minutes.
3. Thank the Lord and take a "word."

CENTERING PRAYER

Sit relaxed and quiet.

1. Be in faith and love to God who dwells in the center of your being.
2. Take up a love word and let it be gently present, supporting your being to God in faith-filled love.
3. Whenever you become aware of anything, simply, gently return to the Lord with the use of your prayer word.

After twenty minutes let the Our Father (or some other prayer) pray itself.

The Method of Centering Prayer

Centering prayer, often called "prayer of the heart" or "prayer in the heart," as well as "prayer of simple regard" or even the "prayer of simplicity" or of "recollection," is an expression of a living tradition. The monks of St. Joseph's Abbey (Spencer, Massachusetts), who have done much to bring this tradition to the United States, have presented it practically in these three simple points.

Generally in the West little attention has been paid to posture in meditation. Practioners of centering prayer are encouraged to find a good chair that keeps the back straight and supports it well, so the energies can flow freely up and down the spinal system; place the feet flat on the floor; and close the eyes gently. If they are familiar with different forms of sitting, perhaps learned from other traditions, they are not discouraged from using them, though they are encouraged not to be dependent on them but keep their freedom to be able to meditate any where, any time, even when such postures are not possible.

The essence of the prayer is in the first point. It is a prayer of being—not thinking, imagining, feeling, remembering or the like, but simply being. In this prayer we do not give God our beautiful thoughts (or ugly ones), feelings, emotions, ideas, images, memories, but just simply we give God our very selves.

Faith is a wonderful gift of God by which we know that whatever God tells us through the revelation is true for God can neither deceive nor be deceived. Jesus on the night before he died told us that "the Father and I will come and make our home in you." God dwells within, in the center of our being. In love we give ourselves to God. This is the whole of the prayer.

In order to stay with the Lord within, this method tells us to use a word, sometimes called a prayer word or sacred word. It is simply a word we choose to serve as a symbol of our intention to consent to God's presence and action within, simply a "yes" to God. The word is not constantly repeated. The prayer word is not a mantra. The word is used only as often as we need it to remain with the Lord.

When we get settled—the body well parked—we turn within and simply rest with the Lord, our word expressing our total intention. Soon enough thoughts (memories, images, sounds, and so on) begin to draw us away from our center. As soon as we become aware of this, we gently—very gently—use our word to return to the Lord. Some days we have to use our word almost constantly for many things are pulling at us. Other days we may not need to use it hardly at all. The frequency does not matter. The thing that matters is our intention to give ourselves completely to God during this time. Beginners are generally encouraged to meditate for twenty minutes, twice a day. Morning and evening mediation is a part of almost every major spiritual tradition. In a world where electricity can change night into day, folks have to find the times most suitable in their lives. Twenty minutes is not sacrosanct. But most find it sufficient time to get some real refreshment (Jesus said: Come to me all you who labor and are heavily burdened and I will refresh you.) but still not too difficult to fit into an ordinary day. Practicality greatly assists fidelity to practice.

We may well settle very deeply into our prayer. So we do advise a gentle return to activity. Jesus has taught us a magnificent prayer—the Our Father—so we usually let this prayer pray itself slowly and gently within, bringing us back to active mind and active life.

This is a very brief presentation of the practice.

Suggested Reading

Benner, David. *Surrender to Love: Discovering the Heart of Christian Spirituality* (Downers Grove, Ill.: InterVaristy, 2004).

———. *Desiring God's Will: Aligning Our Hearts With the Heart of God* (Downers Grove, Ill.: InterVaristy, 2005).

Boylan, Eugene. *Difficulties in Mental Prayer* (Westminister, Md.: Newman, 1943).

Casey, Michael. *Sacred Reading. The Ancient Art of Lectio Divina* (Liguori, Mo.: Liguori/Triumph, 1995).

———. *Toward God. The Ancient Wisdom of Western Prayer* (Liguori, Mo.: Liguori/Triumph, 1989).

Chu-Cong, Joseph. *Contemplative Experience* (New York: Crossroad, 1999).

Cummings, Charles. *Monastic Practices, Cistercian Studies Series* (Kalamazoo, Mich.: Cistercian Publications, 1986).

Finley, James. *Christian Meditation: Experiencing the Presence of God* (San Francisco: HarperCollins, 2004).

Louf, André. *Teach Us to Pray* (Boston: Cowley, 1992).

Keating, Thomas. *Intimacy With God* (New York: Crossroad, 1994).

———. *Open Mind, Open Heart* (New York: Continuum 1986).

Merton, Thomas. *The Climate of Monastic Prayer*, Cistercian Studies Series 1 (Spencer, Mass.: Cistercian Publications, 1969).

———. *The Inner Experience: Notes on Contemplation* (San Francisco: HarperSanFrancisco, 2003).

———. *Opening the Bible* (Collegeville, Minn.: The Liturgical Press, 1970).

Moon, Gary. *Falling for God: Saying Yes to His Extravagant Proposal* (Colorado Springs, Colo.: Shaw Books, 2004).

Pennington, M. Basil. *Awake in the Spirit* (New York: Crossroad, 1993).

———. *Centered Living: The Way of Centering Prayer* (Liguori, Mo.: Liguori/Triumph, 1999).

———. *Centering Prayer* (New York: Doubleday, 1970).

———. *Daily We Touch Him*, 2nd ed. Kansas City, Kans.: Sheed and Ward, 1997).

———. *Lectio Divina: Renewing the Ancient Practice of Praying the Scriptures* (New York: Crossroad, 1998).

Pollard, Miriam. *The Laughter of God* (Collegeville, Minn.: Liturgical Press, 1986).

About the Author

M. Basil Pennington was born in Brooklyn, New York, in 1931, the son of Dale Kelsey Pennington and Helene Josephine Kenny. He entered the Cistercian Order (Trappists) in 1951 at the Abbey of Our Lady of St. Joseph, Spencer, Massachusetts, after graduating from Cathedral College of the Immaculate Conception and was consecrated a monk on September 8, 1956. After ordination to the priesthood in 1957 he spent several years in Rome gaining an S.T.L. and a J.C.L. *summa cum laude*, winning two gold medals from Pope John XXIII. He assisted at the Second Vatican Council as a *peritus* (advisor) and in the preparation of the new Code of Canon Law. With Thomas Merton he started Cistercian Publications in 1968 and founded the Institute of Cistercian Studies at Western Michigan University in 1973. Abbot Basil became known internationally through his efforts to help the Church re-find its contemplative dimension through the centering prayer movement. For four years he served as the vocation father in his abbey, lecturing widely and publishing a book on vocational discernment. In 1983, in collaboration with leaders from other churches and the synagogue, he formed the Mastery Foundation for the empowering of those whose lives are about sacred ministry. From 1986 to 1989 he served at Assumption Abbey in Ava, Missouri. In 1991, he went to help his

Chinese brethren at Our Lady of Joy Monastery, Lantao, where he served until 1998, while continuing his worldwide ministry in centering prayer. He published over sixty books and almost one thousand articles in various languages. Some recent publications are *20 Mysteries of the Rosary: A Scriptural Journey* (2003), *The Abbey Prayer Book: With an Introduction to Cistercian Spirituality* (2002), *Lectio Divina: Renewing the Ancient Practice of Praying the Scriptures* (1998), and *Song of Songs* (2004). Abbot Basil was appointed superior of Assumption Abbey in January 2000 and was elected abbot of the Abbey of Our Lady of Holy Spirit, Conyers, Georgia, the following August. During the last few years of his life, Abbot Pennington retired to the Abbey of Our Lady of St. Joseph, Spencer, Massachusetts—the location where his monastic vocation began.

Abbot Basil died June 3, 2005, at age 74, from injuries sustained in a car accident.